A STRUGGLE WITHIN

THE TRUE STORY OF THE RECOVERY OF A BURN SURVIVOR

By: Lee Lucas

Rodd me
Tell others they can get a copy
of me on Amazon.com

"Long is the way and hard, that out of Hell leads up to light."
John Milton, Paradise Lost

FOREWORD

Our purpose on this Earth is to advance God's Kingdom. We may feel at times that God is slowly growing us to fit that purpose. There may be times in our lives when He needs us to be radically changed.

This true story takes us into a very dark and painful world of one man's transformation. The means of this change that Lee Lucas experienced was beyond human belief. Lee had no control over what happened to him. But Lee's attitude and reliance on the Power of God changed him to become a much better tool for God's purposes for his life.

Each of us will face trials in our lives. No one escapes the trials and tribulations. For some people, there will be physical trials. For others, there will be emotional trials. Financial trials will come about for some. Other people will face periods of loneliness, separation, and even rejection. No one is exempt.

Yet our perception of these trials in your life, and how you persevere through them, is how God refines the ones He loves. Our initial response, when we face difficult circumstances that are beyond our control, is to become angry, have resentment, and great frustration. But God wants you to have enough faith in Him so that you experience His great love in all kinds of situations.

"Consider it pure joy, my brothers whenever you face trials of many kinds, because you know that testing of your faith develops perseverance. Perseverance must finish its work so that you may be mature and complete, not lacking anything." James 1-2 NIV

Lee, his rescuers, his family, his church, and his friends, were called out of their routine, comfortable lives one night to rely on The Power of God through prayer.

As you read the events from many different perspectives, listen for the gentle whisper about how God wants to prepare or change you.

God appeared to Elijah. "After the earthquake came a fire, but God was not in the fire. And after the fire came a gentle whisper." 1 Kings 19: 12 NIV

To hear that "gentle whisper," we must listen intently, and be still from the noise and distractions of our lives. I challenge you to do that as you read this truly remarkable story of one heroic rescue and recovery orchestrated by our Mighty Creator.

Robert E. Foster, M.D

TABLE OF CONTENTS

Introduction

This is the story of my recovery from a traumatic burn injury. It has been written by my friends, my family and me.

In the early morning hours of October 16, 2005, I was caught in a fire. Doctors kept me in a medically induced coma for three weeks. Burns covered 35% of my body, legs, buttocks, stomach, chest, and arms. I had carbon monoxide poisoning with a level of 37.4% and an inhalation injury (burns inside my lungs). I spent a total of 111 days in the hospital. It took over two and a half years for all of my wounds to close and a few more years for my scar tissue to stretch.

Throughout this entire period I was struck by the inspiring outcry of support from my family, friends and many others who we did not know.

The part of this story that I recall is that of

my recovery. Other parts of the story have been pieced together from accounts of those who were there, those who risked their lives to save mine, those who would not leave my side and those who never let me give up hope.

Dedication and Acknowledgements

This story is dedicated to all those who prayed, lent a kind word, sent letters, and comforted my family during those dark days, and to those who believed I would completely recover without any complications.

To my family and friends; to those I have never met who thought of me: thank you for doing me this great service.

I would like to express a special thanks to the brave firemen and paramedics of the Hoover Fire Department in Hoover, Alabama who saved my life. Thank you to all of the doctors and nurses at the University of Alabama at Birmingham Hospital for taking such good care of me, and to the burn survivors who took the time to speak with me about what to expect.

Thank you to my great aunt Doctor Eloise Kirk and our mutual friend, Mrs. Linda Smith who have dealt with my continuous procrastination in getting this story on paper. Thank you to all who reviewed my story and offered their input to help make this book a reality.

I would also like to thank my parents, David and Anne Lucas, who put their lives on hold and did everything and anything within their power to make sure I would completely heal and re-enter society as a productive citizen.

And of course, I offer an extra special thanks to God!

About the Author

My name is Lee Lucas. I've lived in Birmingham, Alabama for my entire life. My parents are, David and Anne. I have an older brother, Brian, who is married to April. They have two daughters, Claudia and Julia. I also have many other loving extended family members.

In the past I have been a competitive bowler in leagues and tournaments throughout the Southeast for many years. I love baseball, playing chess, cooking and reading.

READING THIS BOOK

While reading this book you will see many entries attributed to different authors. Each entry begins with a heading describing who has contributed their narrative.

Many of these are taken from a journal that was kept by my parents and grandparents.

Many entries were written by me. These entries proved to be another form of therapy, allowing me the relief of pouring out my soul by sharing the story of being burned and of recovery.

Some are quotations from historical figures at different points throughout history.

Others are in the form of verses from the Holy Bible. Any verses with the notation NIV are taken from the New International Version; those marked KJV are from the King James Version.

My one request is that you read this book in

its entirety with an open mind before you form an opinion about it. It is the story of my life and recovery.

1. THIS IS THE DAY

ANNE LUCAS, MOTHER

Saturday

On Saturday morning, I participated in a cancer walk at Barber's Racetrack. I had set aside the afternoon to clean my attic. My son Lee had agreed to come over and help, not only because I was paying him to do so, but also because he wanted to sift through the clutter to see what he could take home to his own place.

While cleaning out the attic, one of his tennis shoes came apart at the toes. As he walked the shoe flopped open like a large mouth.

"You need to glue that," I said.

"Then we'd have to wait for the glue to dry. I'll just wrap a rubber band around it and it will be fine." He replied.

I raised my eyebrows from across the attic. His sense of humor often mystified me. I told him that he needed to get rid of the shoes; they will keep falling apart.

Laughingly, Lee replied that they still had a few good years left in them.

I've always thought that he has a warped sense of humor.

"Be sure to throw those shoes away," I shouted as he walked out to his truck.

I have a vivid memory of Lee grinning at me as he flopped out the back door. It stuck in my head-Lee, his shoe held together with a thin rubber band, grinning broadly as he walked, one foot in front of the other, so swift, and so pain-free, out the door.

It would be a very long time before I would see my son walk again.

LEE LUCAS

I helped my mother clean out her attic that day then returned home. In the early evening, I went to my friend Mike's house to watch college football and play some poker.

OWEN, CHILDHOOD FRIEND

I remember all of us at Mike's house for our usual Saturday night poker game. We always met at someone's house to watch college football games and play cards. It was the middle of the Texas Hold'em resurgence.

LEE LUCAS

It would be an early evening for me because every other person there wanted to watch football, not baseball. There was no way I could miss major league playoffs. After poker, football and beer, I headed home to watch baseball.

The time was approximately 9:45 p.m. CST. I got home and watched the ending of the NLCS game 3, St. Louis Cardinals at Houston Astros, collapsed in my bed, and fell asleep.

I woke up three weeks later.

THE PHONE CALL

DAVID LUCAS, MY FATHER

Saturday, October 15, was a beautiful day, sunny and cool. It was perfect weather for an afternoon of football, in fact.

I had left Birmingham early in the morning to head to Oxford, Mississippi with two of my closest friends. We were going to watch Ole Miss play Alabama.

What a game! Alabama kicked a last second field goal to win against Ole Miss. After the victory, my friends and I spent time in the Grove, the legendary tailgating site where fans from both sides gather after every Ole Miss home football game. Tents lined the dirt paths, flags waving. Burgers and sausages smoked on grills. Fans were toasting the victory. People were everywhere, laughing and chanting for our team!

A *New York Times* article once reported that "Ole Miss might lose a football game, but they never lose a party!" The quote resonated in my head that day.

We headed back home well fed and, happy about our victory, but very tired from a long day.

We rolled into Birmingham around 11:20 that night. Before going to bed, I decided to take an Ambien. I was tired, and being overly tired can sometimes interrupt my sleep. I went to bed knowing I would get a good night's sleep before heading off to church in the morning, and fell asleep.

Around 2:15 a.m., I woke up for no apparent reason. I was not groggy. I was not alarmed, just very annoyed. The Ambien had not worked. I glared at the clock and berated myself for waking up. I needed my sleep. I closed my eyes for a second, but remained completely alert.

Suddenly the phone rang.

I reached to pick it up. "Hello?" I said a bit startled.

An ADT operator was on the other end of the line. He quickly explained that the alarm at Lee's condo had gone off. Lee hadn't answered, so he was calling us. At that point I felt a cold fear rush through my body.

The man went on to ask me two questions:

1. How soon could I get to Lee's condo? And
2. What would I be driving?

I was confused. What kind of questions were these? I quickly answered. "We'll be there in five minutes in a red Chevrolet pick-up truck!"

Overhearing my words, my wife leaped out of bed and began dressing. She did not have a clue about what was going on, but she sensed the urgency.

I held the phone closer to my ear as the man from ADT said something that I shall never forget. "Mr. Lucas, I'll give the description of your truck to the police. The roads will be blocked. There have already been several 911 calls to your son's address. But you will be allowed to enter."

I was suddenly filled with a cold fear unlike anything I had known before.

I set the phone down with much haste and Anne and I dressed quickly. I have no idea where I got my clothes from or what I put on, except that I was wearing a baseball cap. During the thirty seconds it took for us to get to the door, I repeated what the man from ADT had shared with me. All I remember was Anne exhaling sharply.

We ran down the steps, side by side, as fast as we could go. We jumped into my truck.

There have been a few times in our lives when we have gotten "middle of the night" phone calls that were legitimate. Most were handled with conversations to calm the one calling in the middle of the night.

I will never be able to explain my sense of urgency that night while driving. God, Himself, helped me drive that short distance from our house to Lee's condo. And it was God, Himself, who would help me get to the hospital.

We crossed the steep ridge behind our house and plummeted down the road on the other side. I never slowed for stop signs.

We screeched to a halt at the roadblock one street away from the entrance to the condo. We jumped out of my truck, leaving it in the middle of the road. I'm not sure if I even turned it off. As we sprinted to the parking area in front of Lee's building, we saw a raging inferno growing in front of us. What we saw made us sick.

All eight condos in Lee's building were on fire. The image, like Hell itself, burned itself on the inside of my mind forever. Flames bathed every outer wall, literally creating their own wind as they forced themselves through every crack in that building. And that huge fire roared.

Pine trees around the building were swaying and popping. The heat was so intense that we felt the heat as soon as we neared the parking area. There were several fire trucks and a huge gathering of observers.

I stared at the building, horrified. Was he home? My eyes scanned the parking lot. Then I saw it. Lee's car was in the corner of the parking lot. His car stood out from the others. It was where he always parked.

We were stopped in the parking lot by a Hoover policeman who would not allow us to go any further. We both began to yell that we thought our son was in his condo. He asked if we had checked the throngs of observers. We had not.

Anne and I split up. We made a fast run past the clusters of people, shouting for Lee as we ran. "Lee! Lee Lucas!" we shouted over and over again. "Lee!"

We returned to the policeman, panicked at the sight of one another without Lee. I told the policeman that Lee was not outside, but his car was. The officer went directly to the firefighters and told them that Lee was inside the condo. One fireman ran over to us and asked where Lee's bedroom was located. We told him that Lee should be down the hall to the right after going in the front door. His bedroom was down toward the end of the hallway on the left. The firemen acted as if they were familiar with the floor plans in this condominium complex.

The firemen ran toward the condo in all their heavy gear. We stood at the edge of the parking lot, feeling the heat of the fire, hearing the roar and watching the flames spread right before our eyes.

In that instant, the first since the phone call, we felt totally helpless. We could only stand, watch, and wait. We held onto each other. Anne began to pray aloud.

One fire truck was parked directly between us and the condo, blocking our view of the inside. I looked desperately over the truck at the balcony of Lee's unit.

I saw the tops of the firemen's helmets as they entered Lee's balcony. That scene is permanently etched in my mind.

The fire was so intense and so bright that I could only see silhouettes-silhouettes of those heroes outlined against the flames. I could see that the firemen were inching forward, entering the door. "Please, Lord, let them find Lee before it's too late," I prayed desperately.

As I watched, the silhouettes changed and faced each other. One silhouette went out of sight. There it was again. I realized that they had picked someone up. It had to be Lee!

"They found him!" Anne and I held tightly to each other.

We saw Lee being carried between those great firemen! Then the silhouettes disappeared behind the fire truck. A fireman ran over and asked if one of us would like to ride in the ambulance. Anne ran with the fireman. I ran to my truck. I stopped to take one last look at the condo.

At that moment, the walls closed in from one end of the building to the other. The condo began to collapse, shooting flames skyward. One more minute, just one, and no one could have entered or exited that building. Another minute would have been too late for our son. It was a miracle that they found him in time, but my deepest anxiety was that I did not know if he was still alive.

I turned and continued running for my truck. I heard the screaming of the ambulance's siren as it exited the parking lot, headed for UAB Medical Center.

I jumped in and I went in high-speed reverse away from the roadblock. I stomped on the brakes, then turned and jerked forward, flying around the roadblock.

I drove to Lorna Road as fast as I could. Then I saw it, the bright, flashing lights of Lee's ambulance. It was right over my head as it crossed the interstate. There was a huge lump in my throat.

I turned on my emergency flashers and I accelerated to over ninety miles an hour. I was determined to catch up to that ambulance that carried my son and my wife.

Adrenaline racing, I made three cell phone

calls as I drove: the first to my parents, the second to our daughter-in-law, April, and the third to our pastor, Brother Scott.

As we exited the freeway and drove onto the city streets, I crept closer to the ambulance. I sailed through every red light that they went through, staying as close as possible-too close, probably.

I was never so thankful to see UAB hospital!

T. LAWSON
FIREFIGHTER/PARAMEDIC
HOOVER FIRE STATION #4
ENGINE 4

The night was like most others, peaceful and quiet. I prepared to rest for the night at the fire station. Sometime after midnight, the call came in to the station. Fire was showing, the voice on the radio cracked, and it was a multiple alarm apartment building fire. I ran toward the engine, glancing at my watch. This was not a good time for a fire of this size. Sleeping occupants might be trapped.

We roared out of the station, lights flashing, sirens on. Engine one called over the radio that they could see the fire from their station. I listened to my captain as he developed a game plan for us in the truck.

We arrived on the scene. I was awestruck at the size of the flames. *How does a fire get this far ahead of us?*

As I stepped off the engine, our driver pointed the monitor gun at the building and unloaded a barrage of water. Nothing seemed to slow the intensity of the flames. A car in the front parking lot was starting to catch fire. All the trees on the front side of the building were bursting into flames; even the pine straw that had been piled around the trees was on fire.

My crew tried to make entry up the front stairwell to attack the fire on the second story, but the stairs were beginning to fall in. At that point, my captain ordered us to set a ladder to the second floor to attack the main body of the fire with hand lines. Several other firefighters, police officers, and I moved the ladder to the front right side of the building. Several of us ran up the ladder and gained entry to the balcony.

I began fighting the fire in an apartment to the right with firefighters Morton and Conlee. Captains Null and Burgess went to an apartment on the left and began fighting there. We were attacking the super heated flames with hand lines.

Over the radio we learned from a fellow fireman that someone was unaccounted for. My heart sank; the conditions we were facing were not survivable for someone without fire survival gear. I asked Morton what he thought about doing a quick search.

"Let's go!" he shouted. At this point, roof truss collapse was beginning to take place. We had a considerable fire attack still underway, and we had to hurry if we were to do a search. Even as a fireman you feel fear, but you learn that there is a greater calling to serve by attempting to save the life of another. On this basis we pushed forward with hope through a situation we knew was not survivable.

As we entered Lee's apartment, we hurried to the right and down a hallway to a bedroom. While Morton searched that room and a closet,

I took a left down a short hallway. And that's where Lee Lucas entered my life.

"He's here!" I shouted. "He's here!"

Lee was lying on his back, his legs folded backwards underneath him. His shins were facing the floor; his stomach was facing the ceiling. He was lying in about three inches of water, halfway between his bedroom and the hallway. Through the smoke and haze, I checked for breathing. To my surprise, he was alive. Morton made his way toward us and shined his light over Lee's body. We glanced over him; there was no entrapment. But there was no doubt that he was heavily burned. I could feel the heat of the water through my boots.

We grabbed Lee by the shoulders and feet and carried him down the hallway. After what seemed like a lifetime, we made our way to the balcony.

Morton screamed for assistance. Captains Null and Burgess helped us get Lee over the railing and down to the ground. I remember watching them put him into the ambulance, which soon roared out of sight. If this guy made it through the next hour, I thought, it would be a miracle.

I was very tired. I didn't know if I could make it over to the rehab area, but I did.

Soon, the other firefighters brought word that the huge fire that had gotten out of control so quickly was out. It turned out that several people had been saved that night.

It was later determined that Lee had been in the fire for approximately 35 to 40 minutes.

I believe that the decisions our officers made during the first few minutes of the fire enabled us to save Lee and the others.

Obviously, God was in control. We cannot and should not attempt to limit Him or His Great Power.

ANNE LUCAS

"Do you want to ride in the ambulance?" someone called.

"Yes!" I shouted. "Yes! Thank you!"

I ran for the ambulance as fast as I could. My heart had been racing, but suddenly it seemed paralyzed with fear. I was helped into the front seat as David turned and ran for his truck.

How can this be happening? I asked myself.

M. Norman, a paramedic, was giving Lee oxygen. He encouraged me from the back of the ambulance: "He's breathing some on his own. That's good."

When I looked back, I saw the top of Lee's head. He was lying still as a stone. There were black burns on his arms, stomach, and the fronts of his legs-ugly black burns with raw, red skin. I was numb, as if I were living a nightmare. It was beyond my comprehension. I turned and looked forward, then flipped around and looked backward in disbelief.

Just yesterday, in the hot attic, I had been with Lee as he was laughing, rubber- banding his shoe. My mind went in circles. Was he wearing the shoe with the rubber band? Is the shoe with the rubber band in the trash, or is he really going to wear it for another year? I turned backward again, realizing how ridiculous it was to care about Lee's shoes at a time like this.

We arrived at the hospital. Someone interrupted my thoughts to give me directions: "Please stay right here until we move your son into the emergency room."

I nodded my head, shaking with fear. I sat, wringing my hands, praying. "Okay," I whispered, "Okay."

Lee was rolled into the hospital. Someone helped me out of the ambulance. I could hardly move. I felt like I had been burned, too.

A nurse took me down a hallway into a little room. I felt cold and I was shaking like a leaf. Someone brought me a warm blanket, but I still shook out of control.

As is sat, people began arriving at the hospital: my husband, David, my daughter-in-law, April, and David's parents soon all rushed in. April's older brother had been called to watch our granddaughters, since our oldest son, Brian, was out of town.

I have no idea how long we waited. We were praying, crying, sitting, standing, pacing, propping, and holding onto each other for dear life.

After what seemed like an eternity, the news was given to us. It was not the worst possible, but very close to it.

Lee had sustained second, third and fourth degree burns over thirty-five percent of his body.

His lungs were damaged from super-heated smoke and carbon monoxide poisoning. His carbon monoxide level was 37.4%.

We looked blankly at the doctor. If a person smoked several packs of cigarettes a day, the doctor explained softly, and lived in the downtown area of a heavily congested city, they might have a carbon monoxide level of 2%. Lee's was 37.4%! I'll never forget those numbers.

Lee's doctors gave us no hope. If Lee lived, and "*if*" was the operative word, they stressed, he might never be able to function normally again. He would probably have severe brain damage.

"Oh, my God! No!" I heard myself shouting over and over again. "No!"

We collapsed together and cried. We were waiting to wake up from this horrible nightmare, but we never did.

Two hours later, at 5:00 a.m., we were taken to the ninth floor of the North Tower where the Trauma Burn Intensive Care Unit (TBICU) waiting room is located. So, this was where our son, Lee, would wait peacefully for his Lord and Savior to take him home.

More people came. Friends from our church were gathering for our son. "How did they hear about this so quickly?" I asked.

HOWARD AND ZENOBA LUCAS (PAPA AND NANA), GRANDPARENTS

That Sunday morning, we received a shocking phone call from our son, David. Lee had been badly burned at his condo. He was being transported to UAB hospital by ambulance. David spoke with obvious terror in his voice. We hung up and were led to pray together. We got dressed and rushed to UAB emergency. Upon arrival, we were taken to where David and Anne were sitting, huddling, waiting for news.

Lee's doctor finally spoke to David and Anne near his emergency room. He relayed that Lee was alive and that every effort was being made to keep him alive, but he did not think Lee was going to survive.

Anne looked straight at him and said, "We don't know about that. We will have to talk to the Lord about this."

AUNT SHIRLEY

With sirens screaming in the background, my sister Anne called to tell me what had happened. I woke my mother, Lee's grandmother, and breathlessly relayed the news. She immediately began to pray for God to perform a miracle and heal Lee.

DOCTOR DAVIDSON, ANESTHESIOLOGIST, CHURCH MEMBER

When Lee was brought into the E.R., he was unconscious. He was not breathing. The paramedics had been helping him breathe with a bag and facemask. As soon as he was wheeled into the trauma bay, he was immediately intubated by the on-call trauma surgeon.

Lee was resuscitated. I.V. fluids were pumped into his body to keep his blood pressure up. Pure oxygen was pumped into his lungs by ventilator to try to overcome the carbon monoxide poisoning.

Lee's burns were estimated to be around 40% of his total body surface area. This, combined with the severe inhalational burn injury to his lungs, made the prognosis very poor.

Another worrisome factor was that Lee had been without sufficient oxygen for a long time, at least until the paramedics arrived, and probably until he was intubated in the E.R.

Fact: anoxic brain injury is irreversible.

All of the doctors involved in Lee's care predicted that he would have brain damage even if his body survived the burns.

THE NINTH FLOOR

DOCTOR FOSTER, CARDIOLOGIST, CHURCH MEMBER

When my wife and I received the call that Lee had been burned, we immediately called several brothers and sisters in Christ. Then, we drove to the Burn Unit at UAB Hospital. Once several family members and friends had arrived, we were told that we could see Lee. This struck me as strange. Lee had been in his bed less than one hour, there were no nurses or doctors around, and I knew he was very susceptible to infection at this time. He needed critical intensive care. Why were we being allowed to enter the room?

The message was clear, I realized, heart sinking. Lee was not going to survive. We were being invited to see Lee alive for the very last time.

What occurred early that morning was the first miracle that I witnessed during this tragedy. In yellow scrubs, gloves and facemasks, we stood around Lee's bed. Arm in arm, we prayed for Lee-not just the prayer of one, but the prayers of many. Our prayer was bolstered by the support of Lee's entire family, his church family, and by the faith that his friends and family had, who were in their homes and in their beds.

All the prayers from near and far formed a lightning rod that channeled the power of God into Lee's badly burned body. It was His power that allowed Lee to survive his external injuries and the burns to his lungs that were much worse than the external wounds.

BRIAN LUCAS, BROTHER

I arrived at the hospital around 5:00a.m., on Sunday morning. I had received a call that woke me up at the hunting club shortly after 3:00 a.m. When I arrived, we were taken back to see Lee. There were about thirty people in his room. They were all wearing those yellow lunchroom lady gloves, caps, and gowns, and they were all praying.

DONNA, FAMILY FRIEND, CHURCH MEMBER

After the family and others arrived at the hospital, the doctors allowed everyone in the waiting room to see Lee. But first, we put on the yellow: yellow gowns, yellow gloves, and yellow masks.

I didn't know what to expect. I didn't understand why we were allowed to go to Lee's bedside; something told me that this didn't make sense. If Lee was so critical, they should only let Anne and David go see him, briefly, then the doctors and nurses should spend time caring for him. I was confused.

We all gathered, about thirty men and women. We made a big circle around Lee's bed. We held hands. Bob led us in a beautiful prayer. I remember the desperate cries from Anne and David while Bob prayed.

I also remember that sea of yellow, yellow gowns being held tightly together by yellow gloves, bound by Christ's unconditional love.

I remember Lee flinching and fighting against the respirator in his lungs. I remember the soot that discolored his nose and mouth. I remember not knowing who anyone was behind those masks and gowns, but feeling that somehow it didn't matter. The beautiful tear-filled eyes were full of love and compassion. That's what mattered.

Then it hit me. I realized why we were allowed to come into the critical care burn unit. Lee was going to die. It was just a matter of time. He was dying in front of us.

DOCTOR BANKS, GYNECOLOGIST AND SUNDAY SCHOOL TEACHER

That Sunday did not start as it normally did. I was having a cup of coffee and finishing up my preparations for the Sunday school lesson when I was interrupted by a phone call that would change the course of a student's life and my own views of prayer. It was the call most dreaded by a friend and feared by a parent. I could not imagine how Anne and David felt. My heart sank and a strange nausea flooded my body.

Sandy, my wife and class co-teacher, kept repeating "Who is it?" She knew from my reaction that this news would be bad.

"It's Lee. He's been burned. They don't know if he will live."

She responded only with, "Where is he?"

I told her that he was at the UAB trauma burn unit. She went to her closet and began to put on hospital clothes rather than church clothes. We were in total disbelief. We hoped that somehow we would find something different at the hospital than what we feared.

The trip to UAB was one the two of us had made many times. I had been a resident physician there for four years. Sandy had been there as a nurse in the intensive care nursery during those same years.

When we arrived at the TBICU, we found other members from our church there as well. Two members of a prayer group that met every Wednesday, Doctor Foster and Doctor Watterson were there. Soon after we arrived, all the church members in the waiting room were invited to go in to see Lee. Sandy grabbed my hand and said, "This isn't good." I had the same thought, and knew that as an experienced ICU nurse, she was right. We would not be invited into a room that was meant to have limited visitors, to keep down infection, if they expected Lee to live.

We entered the room and found Lee lying perfectly still on a bed covered in white bandages. The minimal overhead lights were the only things illuminating the room. Sandy whispered, "I'm afraid they think he's going to die. Just a ventilator, too many of us in the room, and not many I.V. pumps." She always judged illnesses and care by the number of IV pumps. In this case, there were only three. Lee's nose and mouth were coated in charcoal-colored soot. His body appeared otherwise lifeless except for the movement of his chest created by the ventilator. The scene was surreal. Anne asked us to pray. It struck me that this room was as quiet and still as a place of worship.

Doctors Foster, Watterson and I began to pray aloud. We prayed for every aspect of Lee's body. First, we prayed for his individual bodily cells. Then, we prayed for each of his organ systems. You could feel the presence of God. I have never felt the Spirit as strongly as I did in that hospital room. There was a desperate and focused request for God's will to be done as well as the request to help us understand His will and His answer.

We left the room with tears in our eyes, but from the hush, I knew everyone felt as strongly as I, that we had been in the presence of God. This was an odd place to feel His presence, in a room whose silence was broken only by the sound of a rhythmic ventilator and tearful sobs.

G. BURNS, BURN CHARGE NURSE, CHURCH MEMBER

I first became aware of Lee's situation when I saw Doctor Foster and Doctor Banks, who told me that Lee was in the TBICU. I called the TBICU charge nurse on call to ask for details. I was told that it was looking badly for my friend. I went to the waiting area and spoke to a member of the nursing staff who was taking care of Lee. The thing that sticks in my mind, still, was his carboxyhemoglobin level (carbon monoxide level of his blood). Lee's level was 37.4%. During my time in the ER, it was well known that any burn patient with a carbon monoxide level of 20% or higher would suffer neurological damage. Accompanied by his severe lung injury, Lee's prospects were very slim.

I remember thinking there was no way that he could survive. There was medically nothing we could do for him, but we could pray. From the nurse on call, I learned that Doctor's Banks, Foster and Watterson had begun to pray for Lee in a most peculiar manner. They were praying for his individual cells. They were praying for his respiratory cells to do the simple task for which they were designed, despite the terrific injury which they had sustained. I found this to be genius.

DOCTOR WATTERSON, RHEUMATOLOGIST, CHURCH MEMBER

Early that morning, I received a call from Lee's mother, Anne. It was bad news. Lee had been involved in an apartment fire and had been severely burned.

The unforgettable call was one from a family of believers in God to His waiting army. It was for Lee and for our help at that very moment.

My wife, Ruth, and I dressed and headed downtown in the darkness of the early morning. We had trouble locating a parking spot outside the hospital because so many church and family members had already gathered.

We went upstairs. We heard that prospects for Lee's recovery were not good, and as we all gathered, we were being called to act as prayer warriors. Many of us were allowed into his small ICU room, gowned and gloved, which I knew was a major breach of protocol.

I'll always remember the feeling in that room. I'll always remember that there was a feeling that something needed to be done, to be accomplished; it was something that had not yet been accomplished on a spiritual level. Something was out there for us to grab hold of and to take for our own. That something was the omnipotent power of healing that is only in the hands of the living God, the power to bring about a miracle, which only He could do. I looked at my brothers and sisters in Christ in that room. We knew what we were there to do. We were there to PRAY! We were there to call upon the living God.

I remember hearing the doctors go over the medical data on each of Lee's organ systems. Based on the carboxyhemoglobin numbers, it looked like Lee was very likely to have central neurological damage. His respiratory status was compromised significantly. There was probably "third spacing" (a condition that leads to serious problems such as edema, reduced cardiac output, and hypotenstion) at that point, and there was concern regarding hemo-dynamics, infection, and other problems. A group of us, as physicians, were aware that these issues were coming together. I looked at our pastor at Liberty Park Baptist, Brother Scott, and saw in his eyes a look of anticipation and resolve to enter this fight for the Lord.

We gathered together in a Holy embrace and we prayed. We prayed, pouring out everything in ourselves. We prayed with the faith the Lord gives. I felt then and there that the Holy Spirit had accomplished something in return for our obedience to Him.

AUNT PATTY

I remember very clearly receiving a phone call from Papa (Lee's grandfather). His voice was broken as he told me the events that had occurred. As an aunt who had seen Lee from birth, and as a nurse who knew the gravity of the situation, I tore off toward the hospital as fast as I could.

Upon arrival, I was ushered in with loving family members and friends. A sea of yellow gowns with masks and distraught eyes surrounded the bed. There must have been thirty people in the hospital room at that hour.

We were sending pleading prayers up to our Heavenly Father. Seeing Lee in that ICU bed, I felt powerless to help. So, I prayed a silent prayer for Lee as we called upon the Great Physician, our God. It was a very scary time. It made me shudder to think of my precious nephew lying there, with soot all over him, fighting for his life.

DOCTOR WATTERSON

After leaving the ICU room, I had a conversation with a Christian brother, Doctor Davidson, chief anesthesia resident, who amazingly and fortuitously was on burn service at that very moment. Doctor Davidson privately filled me in on some details pertaining to Lee's medical presentation. He pulled me aside and stated sadly that Lee had no prospects for recovery. He said that Lee's condition was not survivable.

Doctor Davidson motioned to me that we needed to talk privately.

We went down a short hallway in the Burn Unit and entered a stairwell. We stood in the stairwell. He turned to tell me that unless God intervened, Lee would face a slow decline probably over a few days to weeks before an unavoidable death.

As we talked in the stairwell, we were led to pray together. We went to that place where nothing is impossible. We prayed to the One with whom all things are possible. We prayed and we prayed. We poured out our souls and we prayed. When we finished our prayer, I looked down and saw where our tears had soaked the steps below us.

AUNT KATHY

At 2:45 on Sunday morning, I woke up with a startle. I felt that something was wrong, I felt an overwhelming need to be with God. So, I prayed for God's will to be done.

Around 5:00 a.m., Papa called. He could hardly talk, he sounded scared to death. I asked if anyone was hurt.

"Lee!" he gasped. He told me that Lee had been in a fire.

My blood ran cold.

My husband Scott went to the hospital. I went to my Sunday school class to teach The Word of God at a time of great fear and unrest within our family. We had a prayer time just for Lee. My son, Chris, told the class that his cousin was burned badly. We didn't know if he was going to live. That class of eleven year olds prayed with all their hearts.

After church, Scott went home to get a mask and his hunting boots, but he was not going hunting. He was going to Lee's condo. We started smelling the smoke a block from the scene. When we got there, we found firemen all over the scene, including one who had gone to high school with Scott.

When I saw the front of Lee's apartment, I wondered aloud how anyone could have survived in that heap of charred wood and metal. Scott finally bothered the fire inspector so much that he let him into Lee's unit, accompanied by a fireman, to gather some of his things. Scott gathered some of Lee's belongings and threw his lockbox out of the window.

As I watched, a crowd gathered to stare in awe at the devastation. A media truck was there too.

Afterwards we went to the hospital, where enough people had gathered to fill the entire waiting room. We were then allowed to see Lee. I take care of coma patients all of the time as a nurse, but it was devastating seeing my nephew like this. We talked quietly and prayed over Lee.

That night, Scott and I took the things from Lee's apartment to his parents' basement. We saved all we could from the charred remains.

DOCTOR LYTLE, PEDIATRICIAN, CHURCH MEMBER

I was on call the weekend of Lee Lucas' fire. As a pediatrician, I am used to getting calls in the middle of the night. But this call was different. It wasn't one of my regular patients. This was a Christian brother from our church.

When I arrived in the ICU Burn Unit, David and Anne Lucas and many other church members greeted me with smiles that, though loving, were bathed in fear and doubtful unrest.

I was asked by Anne to go visit Lee in the ICU to see his condition and pray over him. He was on a ventilator, and he already had many sets of tubing inserted into parts of his body. I knew right away that Lee would only survive by a true miracle from God and constant prayers being lifted on his behalf. Several of us prayed right then. We wanted to stay strong, so we prayed without doubt, but cautious not to give the family false hope.

BROTHER SCOTT, PASTOR AT LIBERTY PARK BAPTIST CHURCH

Sometime before 3:00 a.m. on Sunday morning, I was shaken from my sleep by the voice of our church administrator, David Lucas, on the line. All he said was, "Lee's been in a fire, and they do not think he is going to make it." I hurriedly asked where they were and assured him that my wife, Beth, and I would be right there.

On the way to the hospital, I called several church leaders who woke from their sleep and promised to be there soon. Upon arriving at UAB, we made our way to the trauma burn waiting room, where we found David and Anne, along with a handful of others.

As the sun started to rise, more people began to join us in the waiting room. We waited for word from the medical team while praying for God to intervene miraculously in Lee's life at that moment.

After we received less than encouraging news about Lee's condition, that aside from his burns, the carbon monoxide level in his blood was such that it would either kill him or give him permanent brain damage, we were, to our amazement, allowed to go in and visit. Deep down, I knew they were really allowing us all in to say goodbye. As we pressed into the room, we saw Lee for the first time with a ventilator tube down his throat and machines keeping him alive.

I do not remember who it was, but someone began to lift Lee up to the Father in prayer. The feeling of dread in the room seemed to be replaced by the unmistakable, almost palpable, presence of the Holy Spirit. The prayer that was lifted up was not one of saying goodbye to a brother, but rather one of confident thankfulness for Lee's healing.

I asked two of our church ministers, Stephen and Nate to go back to church and lead the 8:30 a.m. service.

WORSHIP

BROTHER STEPHEN, MINISTER OF EDUCATION AT LIBERTY PARK BAPTIST CHURCH

"Hello," I said to the caller in the wee hours of the morning, struggling to make my raspy voice heard over the line. It took a brief moment for my thoughts to clear enough to understand who I was talking to, and why they were calling so early in the morning. As a minister, and as a general rule, it is never good news on the other line when a call is received at that time of night. My dread was confirmed when I was told that my former youth group member and now friend, Lee Lucas, had less than a 10%chance of survival.

BROTHER NATE, ASSOCIATE PASTOR AT LIBERTY PARK BAPTIST CHURCH

I awoke to the annoying sound of a pounding fist on my apartment door. Irritated, I went to find out who wanted me so early in the morning, and what could possibly be so urgent. I looked through the peephole. There stood my church friend, Mark. I quickly unbolted the lock and opened the door.

Mark said hurriedly, "Lee Lucas' condominium burned down. He's been taken to UAB in an ambulance."

I changed clothes and hurried to the hospital. Once there, I found several church members huddled in the waiting room where I found out Lee had a very minimal chance of living. I could not believe it.

Stephen and I were soon sent back to church to lead the 8:30 a.m. service. Neither of us knew exactly what to do at a time such as this. Neither of us knew what to say. By now, news of the fire had spread throughout the church community. The congregation was expecting a message, an answer, but Stephen decided instead to ask the congregation to pray.

BROTHER STEPHEN

As our 8:30 service commenced, we sang a couple of songs we had planned to perform previously. The remainder of the service we dedicated to prayer for Lee and the Lucas family. People split into small groups for prayer. Afterwards, many came to the altar and knelt, praying individually.

CONNIE B, CHURCH ORGANIST

When my husband, Lee, and I got the call, it was a complete shock! Lee headed to the hospital as I headed to church to play the service. I bumped into a good friend, and the church pianist, Cynthia, as I came through the entrance. We both were in shock! How could we go through the motions of a "prepared" service at a time like this? However, it soon became apparent that the service would act as a "call to prayer."

I cannot say anything else about the service

other than we prayed, and we prayed. It is the natural response of God's people in a situation that was out of anyone's control, but His. It was a time of crying out to God for mercy and grace and healing. It was a response that would be repeated many times, in many different places, and many different ways among God's people for Lee and his family in the days to come.

During the 11:00 a.m. service, we also had a time for prayer. Again, we sought God as we gathered together, some in their pews and many at the altar, all seeking God's Hand upon the situation.

I went to the hospital after the services concluded. Lee and I were astounded by the number of the people who were there. It was a great outpouring of love and compassion and concern.

BROTHER SCOTT, PASTOR

I made it back to lead the 11:00 a.m. service and gave our congregation an updated status on Lee. I knew that people had learned of Lee's incident during their Sunday school classes, and were seeking some sense of direction. During the regular service, I gave the update and called for prayer.

I cannot say who or how many prayed, or how long we prayed, but the time of prayer was unparalleled in any church experience I have had in my entire life. The prayers were filled with faith and courage. People cried out to the Lord for Lee, David and Anne, and the entire Lucas family. The presence of the Holy Spirit was thick, and His comfort, peace, and encouragement flowed over us.

As God's children cried out to Him, His response was to give us reassurance and a peace that went beyond our ability to understand it.

DOCTOR WATTERSON

Our regular church service at 11:00 a.m. had been called off. The service had turned into a prayer meeting. We were given the opportunity to come to the altar and pray.

I can still remember the exact place where I

was kneeling at the very moment we knelt and prayed as a church. I recall having an absolutely unshakable conviction that it was done. It was taken care of, that I should have faith! I knew at that moment that Lee was going to be absolutely fine.

FAITHFULNESS

AUNT SHIRLEY

I called the bowling alley and asked to speak with the manager. I introduced myself and told him what had happened. I asked if he would call Lee's bowling buddies and let them know what had occurred.

JOHN, MY BOWLING AND CHESS BUDDY AND, CHILDHOOD FRIEND

I got the call from Keith, the manager of the bowling alley, saying that Lee had been burned and was in the hospital. The doctors didn't think he was going to make it. I was stunned. After I hung up, I stood in one place for a while, motionless, not knowing how to process what he had told me. I climbed numbingly into the shower, saying over and over again to myself that Lee was not going to die. He couldn't die.

When I got to the hospital and saw the look on Lee's dad's face, it scared the crap out of me. His eyes told me everything.

We both started crying. No one was very optimistic about Lee making it because of the amount of smoke he had inhaled, he told me, tears running down his face.

I started finding out the severity of his burns from some of the other visitors in the waiting room, which was horrible. One thing I was thankful about was that the burns were from the stomach down.

LEE S., MY BOWLING BUDDY AND CHILDHOOD FRIEND

When I received the call from Keith, I went into shock. Lee wasn't going to survive? Nothing made sense. It was overwhelming. My wife, Kelly, and I were in a state of complete and helpless shock. I had to go see Lee for myself.

En route to the hospital, my wife and I turned onto Lorna Road to pass by the condominium complex. Lee's condo was gone. There was smoldering ash, some framing, but no windows, just a black burned out and horrifying hollowed structure.

How did he make it out alive at all?

I turned to Kelly and said, "Why Lee?"

To my surprise, the waiting room on the 9th floor in the UAB TBICU unit was packed full of people, most of whom I did not know. As I waded through the sea of unfamiliar faces, I found Lee's parents. I remember grabbing and hugging Lee's mom, Anne, as if she were my own mother. I was there to support her, but I soon found Lee's parents consoling me.

DAVE, MY BOWLING BUDDY AND CHILDHOOD FRIEND

I was in my basement talking to my wife when John called. I knew something was wrong by the way he said, "Hey man." His voice was heavy and full of dread. He said that Lee had been in a fire last night, and we need to get to the hospital immediately because he is probably not going to make it. I hung up and started shaking uncontrollably. I finally found a way to call George to tell him what had happened, and that I was coming to pick him up.

GEORGE, MY BOWLING BUDDY AND CHILDHOOD FRIEND

Dave called me to let me know he was on his way to pick me up to go to the hospital to see Lee, who was probably about to die. When we arrived at the waiting room on the 9th floor, the place was packed. It was amazing to see how many family members and friends were there to support Lee and his family. When we talked to Lee's mom and dad, they told us he was in pretty bad shape.

DAVE, MY BOWLING BUDDY
AND CHILDHOOD FRIEND

When we arrived at the hospital, there were many people in the waiting room for Lee. The news going around was not good. My one clear memory is of Lee S. saying loudly that if anyone could pull through this, Lee could!

I dropped George off, rode by Lee's condo, and found the building destroyed. I pulled to the side of the burnt lawn and talked to a fireman. He allowed me to go into Lee's condo to see if I could salvage anything.

I saw nothing I thought could be saved. I saw where the roof above Lee's bed fell in. I saw where one of my best friends, Lee, had basically cooked for 40 minutes. It felt like a nightmare.

The first night of bowling without Lee was sadly difficult. George and I decided to visit Lee before we bowled every single week.

JASON, MY CHILDHOOD FRIEND

I was with my future wife, Sherice, at church on the north side of Birmingham. My phone rang and it was John, a mutual friend to Lee and me. When I stepped out into the hall to answer, his voice was shaking as he told me, "There was a fire in Lee's condominium last night, and he is in the ICU at UAB. We are all here. You need to come here right now!"

On my way to the hospital, my thoughts raced. Just two days earlier, Lee had come over to my house to grill steaks and watch the White Sox beat the Angels, 5-2 in the ALCS. In Birmingham Alabama, we have the Birmingham Barons which is the AA affiliate of the Chicago White Sox. Lee and I used to watch, in person, future MLB players such as Frank Thomas, Robin Ventura, Bo Jackson, and Michael Jordan play baseball for the Barons.

When we got to the hospital that morning, the waiting room was packed full of people. We were there all day. Before we left, I learned from Lee's parents that he had come home Saturday evening and must have fallen asleep before the fire started. He had been rescued by firemen who found him bathed in flames. He had been placed into a medically induced coma. Lee's parents asked us to pray.

I thought of Lee, prayerfully confident that he would pull through. But I also couldn't stop thinking about what was happening on the inside to Lee, who had no feeling at this point, no idea of what had happened, and no idea of what was in store for him when and if he eventually woke up.

AWESOMENESS

MY GRANDPARENTS PAPA AND NANA:

Prayer was our best weapon for such a time, not only from us, but from all of our families, church family, friends, co-workers and others. Our prayers for Lee included a special word for the doctors, nurses and other medical personnel as they worked tirelessly to save Lee's life.

TERI, CHURCH FRIEND:

I was out of town, in my motel room, when I heard about Lee's condition. Early that October morning, after my husband, David, called me and relayed the horrible details, I walked outside. A blue fog was lifting off the mountaintops, creating a beautiful scene that stood in stark contrast to the information I was digesting. Sinking down onto the mossy rocks around me, I began the first of many prayers for God to save Lee.

I had come to know Lee just a few months before, on a mission trip in which we shared eye team duty. The eye team was responsible for setting up simple eye testing clinics for reading glasses to distribute to locals. His love for the Lord, his quiet, strong and determined personality, and his tenacity and drive to overcome obstacles were traits I loved about him. We shared the same weird sense of humor, and I liked his, *if I can do it myself, I will,* attitude.

In the beauty of some of God's most glorious creation, feeling so far away from home and quite useless, I poured out a plea to the Creator, the

Creator who had made every one of Lee's cells. "Let him live-let Lee be whole again, and not just whole in his body, but be Lee again, that crazy young man who is not afraid, who loves God and his family and his country with a passion not seen in most his age."

OWEN, MY CHILDHOOD FRIEND:

I was at work, starting an overnight shift, when I received a call from Lee's mom, Anne. She told me that Lee was in the UAB burn unit and might not make it through the night. She asked me to come to the hospital as soon as possible because the doctors did not know how long he would hang on. After I composed myself, I called my lieutenant and asked him if I could leave immediately to see my friend for the last time. He told me that due to a lack of man-power, I could not leave right then, but that I could have the rest of the week off. What followed was one of my worst nights at work. I did not accomplish anything on patrol because all I could think about was my friend. I prayed all night that God would let him live, and that Lee would wake up again.

When I finally got off work, my future wife, Jessica, and I went to the hospital. We were met with a surreal scene. The whole waiting area was full of people. They were gathering in groups, praying, reading the Bible, and crying. I found Mrs. Lucas. We embraced in a long hug and cried. I introduced her to Jessica, and Mrs. Lucas introduced us both to many of the other people in the waiting room. We sat down and prayed with Mrs. Lucas and many others who we did not know. Jessica and I stayed most of the day.

MIRACLE

DOCTOR WATTERSON:

On that first Wednesday after the fire, October 19, Doctor Banks, Doctor Foster and I decided that we would dedicate our small and secluded prayer meeting to Lee and his healing. We got an update on the latest news and the status of his condition on a medical level, which allowed us to pray specifically about things from a medical aspect.

We were about to pray for favorable results of Lee's CT scan and no brain damage when someone's cell phone rang. It was Lee's mom, Anne. She told us that Lee's brain scan came back "stone-cold clear," which was exactly what we were about to pray for.

At that moment all of us had a recollection of the promise in **Isaiah 65 vs. 24 (KJV):** *"And it shall come to pass, that before they call, I will answer; and while they are yet speaking, I will hear."*

Doctor Banks, Doctor Foster, and I committed to hold this private prayer meeting for Lee each Wednesday for as long as needed.

OWEN

Jessica, my future wife, set up a Caring Bridge site, an online journal, for Lee so others could keep tabs on him, and so that his parents could spread prayer requests quickly.

JOURNAL

10/19: results of CT brain scan came back as "stone cold clear," very critical stage of first 72 hours has passed. Mike, bowling buddy and childhood friend of Lee's bowled a 300 tonight and said he dedicated it to Lee.

BRIAN LUCAS, MY BROTHER
THREE DAYS AFTER THE FIRE
PRAYER MEETING AT CHURCH

The smoke detector and ADT saved Lee's life. Lee is currently doing the best he can. Lee is a stubborn fighter, and we just cannot give up hope. We are witnessing a miracle happening. Today, Lee had his CT brain scan which came back, in the words of the doctor, "stone-cold clear." Mom and April were there when the news was delivered. They both said they were shaking when they were told.

Considering that his initial carbon monoxide level was over 37%, this is nothing short of miraculous; from what I have been told, it even defies medical science. Just a few days ago doctors were saying he would have brain damage from the smoke inhalation "if" he survived. Wow!

Mom and Dad are doing the best they can. Mom is happy one moment, sad the next. Dad seems a little worse. Many people are visiting, though, and I think that distraction is what keeps them going. Two to three hundred people have come by so far, visitors who make the days pass quickly.

Lee's temperature upon ER admission was 103.3. Yesterday it dropped to 102.3 and now it is 101. He is responding somewhat to unconscious physical therapy to check his mobility. Even while unconscious he has been making grimacing faces so we know it hurts him, but he has sustained it so far. His pain medication level has been dropped from 3 to 1.

We were able to save some things from Lee's condo. For example, we found a small Bible that our grandfather had carried as he served as a Navy corpsman at the battle of Iwo Jima. The Bible experienced only slight water damage. A Japanese diary that our grandfather found during the Second World War survived untouched. Lee had owned signed baseball cards, hundreds of them, but we were only able to save a few. There were many pictures, small statues, and artifacts that belonged to our grandparents from their time serving as missionaries in Africa were saved, but with smoke and water damage. We feel that most of them can be salvaged. A few chess sets were saved. Lee's autographed baseball memorabilia and framed pictures are unsalvageable.

Many people from the bowling alley have asked about Lee. Thirty or more people call each day asking about his progress.

People from Lee's work place have donated two television sets, a sofa and other items. They are all looking forward, with hope, to his time of recovery.

OWEN

I received a call from Mrs. Lucas who told me that Lee was doing better, and that he might actually make it through. I was very excited! I stopped and praised God right then for having His hand in this.

JASON

A few days after the fire, Owen and I went back to the ICU and saw Lee for a few minutes. Because of the open wounds and risk of infection, we had to wash our hands and put on hospital gowns, gloves and masks. Lee was lying there wrapped in gauze and blankets, with a tube in his mouth and machines attached to him. I cannot describe the emotions I felt at seeing my friend so helpless.

LEE S.

The nurses would only let family back to see Lee, so I was acting as his brother for the day. When I was finally allowed in, I almost asked if it was really him. Lee looked nothing like himself; he looked nothing like I expected. It is hard to describe the feeling and the emotions that were going through my head. I honestly thought it was the last time I would see Lee, and I felt that it was important he knew I was there for him.

My wife, son, and I visited the hospital as

often as we could. We were going to support Lee's parents and to say goodbye to our friend.

However, I was struck by Lee's parents' unshakable faith. The doctors only spoke in "ifs," "if Lee makes it 24 hours he will be a vegetable," "if Lee makes it 48 hours he'll lose his legs," "if... if...if..." But his family said "when." There were no "ifs" only "when's." Unshakable; I was in awe of the miraculous things happening in that hospital.

THAT THE LORD HAS MADE

DAVID, CHURCH FRIEND

Several days after the accident, I recall one of our church greeters breaking down and crying as she talked about the likelihood of serious infection due to Lee's open wounds.

DOCTOR PRESLEY, INTERNIST

I was not able to see Lee for several days. When I saw him I was not only happy to see Lee alive but surprised because he was making progress considering his vegetative state. Lee's extremities were becoming more mobile during his therapy sessions while in a coma, which meant healthy circulation and increased brain activity.

DOCTOR DAVIDSON

While Lee was in the ICU, daily bronchoscopes were performed to remove the burned lung tissue that clogs the airways and promotes pneumonia. Only minimal sedation ordered at first, and Lee was still unresponsive. This was a bad sign.

DOCTOR BANKS

The weeks were filled with prayers. Lee's family was constantly there. Prayer was more important to the family than any physical support given- food for the family or other simple acts of care in a time of need. Anne and David's faith was unbelievable.

DOCTOR LYTLE

Sometimes people ask me, "What is the worst thing that you see in pediatrics?" I usually think of child abuse and neglect first, but the accidents that tug at my heart hardest are child burn patients. Burns trigger the most terrifying screams from innocent children. Adults with burns experience this same type of horrendous pain. Lee was about to find this out for himself.

II. THE FIRE

LEE

The condos I lived in were actually old apartments that had been converted into condominiums. I lived on the second floor of an eight-unit building built in the 1960s. My unit had two bedrooms, two bathrooms, a kitchen, a dining area, a sizeable front porch, and an attic that I shared with other tenants who lived on my floor in that building. I bought the place in January 2002, and had purchased an ADT alarm system when I moved in.

I do not remember any of the following events; I write only based on what has been told to me. In the early morning hours of October 16, a neighbor was cooking something in grease, probably french fries. He left to go to the bathroom, and when he came back, his kitchen was on fire. He tried to put water onto the fire to extinguish it. That water created a mini explosion that spread greasy fire all over the kitchen. The fire made its way into the air ducts and common attic and spread to the other units. It tore through the insulation in the common attic and engulfed my condo along with the rest of the building.

I had apparently gotten out of bed and tried to leave the room, but I was cut down by the smoke. I fell onto the floor under the threshold in the doorway between my bedroom and a short hallway. I fell on my knees and leaned back with my legs underneath me. Pipes in the walls were starting to burst, my water heater was spewing water, and fire hoses had started to rain in through the window and my roof. There was about three inches of water on the floor, and it was becoming hot as fire. I was boiling.

Two brave firemen made their way into my condo in hopes that they would find me. It was a surprise to these honorable brave souls, who felt the heat through their boots, that I was still alive. I was swiftly moved toward safety, then, faithfully passed on to others in the hope that I would live.

I had been in the fire for 35 to 40 minutes.

The fire marshal said that the place where I was found, lying in water under the threshold between my bedroom and hallway, was the best place that I could be to have a chance to survive.

This is because of the building structure and the strength of the roof mounting that was over me. The fact that I was lying in water was good, because water has oxygen in it that helped to preserve my skin and prolong my survivability.

III. ICU

LEE

The following is based on what I have been told and what was recorded in a journal kept by my family during my ICU days.

On October 20, while I was still unconscious, the doctor decided he would start skin grafts using my own skin. This was a great sign because it meant that the doctor thought I might survive. At this time, I was at stage 3 on the Glasgow Coma scale. The scale ranges from stages 3 to 15, 15 being completely alert and functional as an everyday person.

I woke up in the hospital on November 5. By the time I woke up, I had had a skin graft and one major skin debridement. A skin debridement surgery basically consists of a scraping off of dead tissue (debris) or deep cleaning of a wound.

ANNE LUCAS

Patty and I got to see Lee's stomach both before and after his skin debridement surgery. Before the procedure his stomach was completely black, much like a charred piece of meat. After the debridement, Patty mentioned how good and pink his stomach looked. To me his stomach looked like a red moon crater.

LEE

I was burned on my stomach, chest, arms, legs and buttocks. I had second degree
burns on parts of my chest and arms and third degree on my stomach, buttocks and legs. I had fourth degree burns on both of my shins; I would later learn that a fourth degree burn is one that goes down to the bone.

Donor skin used for each skin graft was harvested from my body. A donor site used for the harvesting of skin for a graft creates a second degree burn on the harvested area, according to the head burn doctor, Doctor Cross. This meant that by the time all nine of my skin grafts were completed, I would have burns on 65% of my body; basically more than half of my body was an open wound. Donor skin was harvested from my upper arms, my chest, back, and waist. I had severe inhalation burns in my lungs and a carbon monoxide level of 37.4%. I've been told this means 37.4% of my blood was carbon monoxide.

From a scientific point of view, the process of a skin graft is very interesting. According to Doctor Cross, who performed my skin grafts, a machine cuts a small piece of donor skin, just 1/12 of a centimeter thick, from the harvesting site. The doctor then places this skin into another machine that punches small microscopic holes into it. The size of the donor skin multiplies by as much as three times after the holes have been punched into it. The doctor then sprays fine misty glue over the burned area and places the donor skin onto the wound.

I thank God that I was unconscious during

these procedures. When I woke after each skin graft I found myself wrapped in more gauze, not fully knowing what had happened, with orders not to move.

This order was given because the newly placed skin could detach, and I would have to have another surgery to correct it.

OBVIOUS MEDICAL FACTS

LEE

I was extremely fortunate to not have burns on my feet, back, hands, face or genitals. Considering that the firemen found me lying on my back with my shins facing the floor in about 3 inches of water, it was especially a miracle that my feet and back were not burned.

I try to picture the strange position in which I was found, but I can't. Lying on my back with my shins facing the floor and my stomach facing the ceiling, I was in a strange kneeling position.

It's almost like a statue, pleading and praying for mercy.

JOURNAL

Dates and events during ICU:

10/16: Fire, Lee was admitted to TBICU with severe burns to his body and lungs, carbon monoxide level of 37.4%, very critical condition, liver and other body functions good, was placed on a ventilator.

10/19: Results of CT brain scan came back as "stone cold clear," very critical stage of first 72 hours has passed.

10/20: Lee opened his eyes for the first time.

10/24: Debridement surgery

10/25: Lee has opened his eyes every day since the 20th, but today when he opened his eyes he seemed very scared, as if he did not know what was going on.

10/26: Lee squeezed nurse's hand on command, Lee wiggled his big toe for RN Aunt Patty on command. Lee received a card from the White Sox PR lady stating "Frank Thomas and the 2005 White Sox are pulling for you!"

10/27: Lee responded to questions today by blinking his eyes. Lee opened his eyes wide when told the White Sox won the World Series.

10/28: First skin graft; received word of fellow believers and their church congregations in Venezuela, Honduras, Japan, Australia, and Africa and all over the world were praying for Lee.

11/5: Ventilator successfully removed. He is breathing entirely on his own. Lee moved to step-down trauma burn unit, where meds will be drastically decreased and people can stay with him.

JOHN

When I first saw Lee lying in his bed bandaged, he looked very gnarly. He was bloated to about twice his normal size and it looked like someone went to town on his face with brass knuckles.

GEORGE

Only immediate family members were allowed to see Lee in the ICU unit, so his mom told the nurse I was his brother. When I first saw Lee, his face was swollen and he didn't look like himself. He was unconscious, but his mom asked me to come up with something to say that Lee might recognize and react to. The first thing that came to mind was the James Brown song "Get on the Good Foot." So, I sang to Lee in my best James Brown voice. And his finger twitched.

AUNT KATHY

Many evenings as I sat with Lee in ICU, I would read from a <u>Bible</u> given to him and his family. It had many passages underlined and was left at the bedside for anyone to read. I recall reading the 23rd Psalm into Lee's ear.

Psalm 23 (NIV): *"The Lord is my shepherd, I shall not be in want. He makes me lie down in green pastures, he leads me beside quiet waters,* *he restores my soul. He guides me in paths of righteousness for his name's sake. Even though I walk through the valley of the shadow of death, I will fear no evil, for you are with me; your rod and your staff they comfort me. You prepare a table before me in the presence of my enemies. You anoint my head with oil; my cup overflows. Surely goodness and love will follow me all the days of my life, and I will dwell in the house of the Lord forever."*

G. BURNS, BURN CHARGE NURSE

Time passed and, regardless of obvious medical facts, Lee was surviving and was getting better. Lee slowly regained the chemistry in his body that could sustain life. Time went on and Lee progressed and was sent to the Trauma Burn Nursing Unit (TBNU). This is my unit, the place where I was the night shift charge nurse. I was going to be able to watch his progress day by day.

DOCTOR WATTERSON

From this point, the progress was moving slowly ahead, but ultimately and progressively, Lee improved more and more in his recovery.

DAVE

I finally got to see Lee; I will never forget the look in his eyes. I taped the World Series for Lee because the White Sox were in it, and I wanted Lee to be able to watch it.

IV. Waking up in the hospital

November 5

LEE

On November 5, I had been moved from the TBICU to the step-down TBNU. I recall opening my eyes, realizing that something had happened to me because there was continuous pain, and then being told by my parents that I had been badly burned. I had been unconscious for 21 days while on a ventilator. I recall blurrily staring off into the near distance for several moments thinking, "Wow! 21 days!"

I softly, with a very scratchy throat, asked if the White Sox had won the World Series.

Somehow that was the first thing that popped into my head. After finding out they had won in four games, I remember thinking I wished I had been able to watch it. My parents assured me that Dave had recorded the World Series games for me so I could watch them one day. I also found out that a radio had been placed in my ICU room so I could hear the games while unconscious. The good Lord does have a sense of humor for it had been 86 years since the White Sox had won a World Series, and I was not able to watch it live. I felt strangely jilted.

As I emerged from the haze and my painkillers began to wear down, I began to feel something else-something that shattered any hopes for a walk through life without the screaming horror of a constant and merciless agony.

I could see and feel that I was wrapped in bandages from my mid-chest to my ankles. I had no idea what was going to happen next.

DAVID LUCAS

I stayed the night with Lee on the first evening that one of us could remain in his room. The *Wizard of Oz* was coming on TV. Lee said he wanted to watch it. He started snoring when the tornado came and took Dorothy to Oz. For the rest of the night I was busy keeping Lee from pulling at his medicine ports and other tubing that had been placed on him. I did not get one wink of sleep.

PAIN

LEE

The pain I was feeling was soon my entire world, the only thing that seemed real. Life had become a strange and terrifying dream; I was trapped in a nightmare that was my own reality.

Genesis 49:18 (NIV), *"I look for deliverance, O Lord."*

When I was young and skinned my knee or did something that caused me to feel pain, my dad would say, "It'll feel better when it quits hurting." It's a genius response because it is true. It sets a mind frame, establishes a mental barrier, and gives you an end goal to shoot for in dealing with the pain. And it is very simple. It is not too exciting to hear this when you are going through a lot of pain. But since I had heard it so much growing up, the phrase would sometimes ring out softly beneath the loud, searing pain tearing through my body. *I will feel better when it quits hurting.*

JOE C.,

My family and I brought some Kentucky Fried Chicken and mashed potatoes with all the trimmings for Lee's parents. I knew Lee could not eat solid food, but I was kind of hoping the aroma would seep into his hospital room and encourage his senses to wake up.

LEE

"Why? Why, God, would you allow such a thing to happen?"

There was constant pain with every single movement and even pain when I did nothing. Tubes were coming and going in all directions, horrifying tubes filled with vitamin supplements and for the gathering of human waste. There was a tube for I.V. fluids and pain medication. A central venous line had been put in for the administering of medications and other fluids. All of these were hooked up to an obnoxiously loud machine. I could not yet eat solid food.

There was a constant rumbling hunger, a pain in my stomach that seemed to never be satisfied. There was a constant aching in my soul that was yearning for an answer, a desperate search amongst the cloudy haze of recovery.

The pain screamed through my body. Every time my heart beat, every time I took a breath, there was an unfathomable throbbing and lightning-quick shooting pain. When my heart would beat faster, in a panic from the pain throughout my body, the pain would become more aggressive. When I would breathe hard, it multiplied. When I tried to sleep, the pain was sadistic. I lay there in my hospital bed, tormented, maddened by pain.

Psalm Ch. 130vs. 1(NIV), *"Out of the depths I cry to you, O Lord."*

JOURNAL

11/7: Lee is wide awake, his voice is low and scratchy due to the smoke inhalation and the ventilator. RN G. Burns, who is the head burn nurse, came by to check on Lee, and Lee completely turned his head to see him.

DRESSING

OWEN

I was privileged to be able to stay with Lee for a few evenings so his parents could sleep in their own bed. These were long nights for me, but I knew they were longer for Lee. At this time, Lee could do nothing on his own. All I could do for Lee was call his nurse and pray, because Lee could not move at all from the severe pain. We talked a little bit, but due to the pain medications, the conversations were disjointed (although humorous).

LEE

The pain was horrendous while I lay in my hospital bed. But the pain during my daily burn dressings was something I previously never could have imagined.

I was having daily burn dressings which consisted of a nurse or nurses clipping off my bandages, washing my wounds with soap, and bandaging me up again. The only way I can come close to describing the experience is to say that it was like someone tightly wrapping duct tape around my body in certain areas then pulling it off along with my skin. Next, there seemed to be a sadistic purification in the form of a cleaning of my open wounds. The wound cleaning during these dressing changes made my pain feel like tree sap, thick and difficult to remove, constant and everywhere. It seemed impossible to have any sort of relief during these changes. Lastly came the re-bandaging, which in my mind felt like simply a twisted joke so that someone else could repeat the merciless agony taking them off again. Burn dressing changes are critical for a burn patient. The risk of infection when burn wounds are not cleaned is the number one killer of any burn survivor/patient.

In the beginning, I remember being wheeled into a room on a gurney and being placed onto a table where the dressing change would commence. I was not exactly sure of what was going on and or why someone was causing me so much pain; it was as though I had fallen into a medieval torture pit. Feverishly, I thought of the delusional, mentally ill Nicholas Medina from Edgar Allan Poe's "The Pit and the Pendulum," tying me down to be tormented by the slow descent of a pendulum with a large blade on the end of it. All the while, the faces of my impish tormentors seemed to be lit with a creepy sense of absolute satisfaction. I did not have a clear understanding as to why these people were causing me so much pain. I only knew that I was in my own Hell.

G. BURNS, BURN CHARGE NURSE

There is a procedure that every burn patient goes through called burn dressing. During this time, daily, the patient goes to the hydro-therapy (water treatment) area, where the dressing team strips them of their old dressings and then, for lack of a better term, scrubs and removes the scabs from the burn wounds. It is the most painful procedure that you can imagine. You must understand that some of the patients, during this daily event, plead for us to let them die rather than go through it again.

"Words have no power to impress the mind without the exquisite horror of their reality."
Edgar Allan Poe

THE STORM

JOURNAL

11/10: Lee wasn't very comfortable today but he talked more than usual. His voice is still raspy and soft but his memory and responses are great.

LEE

Throughout the next day with continued burn dressings and physical therapy, there was a constant and damning pain in everything I did. My personal faith felt shattered; I felt I had done nothing to deserve what was happening to me, nor did I completely comprehend what was going on. I was furious with God for allowing this to occur. I questioned all His power and everything I had believed about Him. I was in a very dangerous state of denial; I was in mourning for the life I previously had.

I had an enlightening moment regarding my understanding of denial, of mourning. This moment came through what I was experiencing.

Mourning is very personal and trying, but overall it is healthy. The best way mourning can be described is in the case of the loss of a loved one. There is a realization that things will not be the same anymore. That what once was will never be again.

It is difficult to recognize what is transpiring, but with this recognition can come a sense or a desire to be with one who knows no secession. An aspiration to hold fast and never let go of what you believe-to find a bridge to connect to that which once was with what is possible.

Psalm 37:7 (NIV), *"Be still and wait patiently for him."*

JASON

Lee's parents asked me to stay the night with him so they could get some much needed rest. I gladly accepted, for I know Lee would have done the same for me had the situation been reversed. This was the first time I would see Lee awake since the fire. On my way to the hospital I pondered upon what we would talk about. I had many questions but I was afraid to ask him about the accident.

When I arrived, Lee's parents told me what to expect. His nurse came in to deliver his medications and breathing treatment he needed to rebuild the tissue in his lungs due to his smoke inhalation injury. Lee and I talked for a few minutes about work and my family, and then suddenly, Lee was snoring away. I read a book that had been left in the room about a shepherd boy named David. This book explained how David, a shepherd, appreciated the way the Lord protected him just as he protected his own flock. No matter what storms we have to endure, there is comfort in his message.

THE APPROACH

JOURNAL

11/11: Lee had a swallowing test today, which he failed. We told him that today marked 27 days in the hospital. He took the news quietly, which is very typical of Lee. He was able to drink some water by sucking on a small sponge. We have a small hospital-issued cup and sponge. The cup is filled with water. Someone will dip the sponge into the water then place it into Lee's mouth so he can suck the water out of it. This is a tedious and slow task that Lee cannot stand.

11/12: Lee insisted we call his manager at his workplace to tell her he was in the hospital. We assured him that she knew he was there. Tonight Lee decided it was time to go home. He said "See ya later!" We explained that the doctor wouldn't let him go right now. Lee insisted that the doctor had no idea what was best for him.

LEE

On 11/13, I was visited by the physical therapist who wanted me to get out of bed to try to walk. I was helped onto my side and, managed to stand up, but only with a lot of assistance and a great deal of pain. I next recall deliriously leaning against my father while looking at the floor, watching blood drip out from under my hospital gown. I looked at my dad and started laughing at the dripping blood. His face was as white as a ghost. I thought, *it'll feel better when it quits hurting.*

DAVID LUCAS

Today as Lee was attempting to stand and walk he leaned against me. Blood started to drip onto the floor from under his hospital gown and instead of panicking, Lee just laughed. I felt cold and a little freaked out by his strange and immediate response.

LEE

After being placed back into bed, I prayed: "Oh Lord, why did this happen? Why am I forced to go through this? What is the meaning of it all?"

Exodus 14:13 (NIV), *"Do not be afraid. Stand firm and you will see the deliverance the Lord will bring you today."*

LEE

I first started to focus my mind again by choosing to look at my injury squarely and see it as the greatest of any personal struggle I had ever experienced. I would use what I had learned from bowling and my love of competition. I would use the old saying that 10% of the game is physical and 90% of the game is mental. However, that wasn't entirely complete, I realized. It is true that 10% of the game is physical and 90% of the game is mental, but 90% of the mental game is attitude.

I could choose to look at this time in my life as

a great and devastating defeat and give up, or I could look at is as the closing of one book in my life and the opening of another and keep going.

"Ability is what you're capable of doing. Motivation determines what you do. Attitude determines how well you do it." **Lou Holtz**

DAVE

I was honored when Lee's parents asked me to stay with him on several occasions so that they could go to church. They didn't want to leave him alone for any amount of time in the hospital. While visiting I could hear the pain in his voice. I heard many strange things from Lee. Some things that made me laugh then, and many that make me laugh now. Lee said that if we were ever stranded on a deserted island, he would volunteer to be eaten first because he was already partially cooked.

HEART

TERI, CHURCH FRIEND

I watched Lee on several occasions at night so his family could rest. One of the duties of the night watch was to prevent Lee from pulling out his medicine port (central intravenous line) and help him remember to not scratch and claw at his healing skin. Lee was heavily sedated and would attempt these forbidden activities in his half asleep state. However, Lee spent most of the night snoring at an astoundingly high decibel level; it was only when he awoke occasionally that he needed to be reminded not to touch that tube or scratch his wounds. I was unwilling to close my eyes for a second all night long because, by golly, he was not going to pull out his medicine port or further injure his healing burns if I had anything to do about it.

LEE

A large black man named Melvin, who was my nurse, told me about another man on my floor who had been burned and was in the same unit I was. This individual was not burned nearly as badly as I was, but he remembered being burned. He would wake screaming in horror at his nightmare. Thankfully, I have no memory of being burned. Confused as I was with God's ways, I was grateful for that.

JOURNAL

11/14: We spent a lot of time talking about the fire and the weeks in the ICU (which Lee does not remember). Yesterday afternoon, Lee said a pleading prayer, "Lord, I am sorry for my recent feelings against you, and I don't want to be selfish, but I am so uncomfortable. Please help the pain." Lee's Nana and Papa were with him today. Lee insisted that someone had stolen his check book. Papa assured him that it had been burned, but Lee did not stop asking until he spoke on the phone with his mother, who said she had it. Actually, the checkbook had been burned.

LEE

I always made it a point to be as polite as possible to all who were taking care of me, whether it was a doctor, nurse, therapist, family or friend. My reasoning behind this was that I knew doctors, nurses, and therapists could cause me more pain if they wanted to (even though it would be against medical ethics). I was polite to my family and friends because they were sacrificing their own time and lives for my comfort.

JOURNAL

11/15: Lee continues to say off-the-wall things, but with a good and alert memory. He is still very well mannered while evidently in great pain. He thanks his nurses every time they visit and even when they perform burn dressings and therapy. He is still a real "southern gentleman." All his nurses say he is their favorite patient. Lee's dependence upon God's leading and his personal determination is very inspiring to us.

PAPA AND NANA

It was natural for us to empathize with the pain and suffering that Lee was undergoing. We have experienced times when we had to rely completely on the Lord, and it was a relief to know that he was finding comfort in God too.

"We shall draw from the heart of suffering itself the means of inspiration and survival."
Winston Churchill

BREAKTHROUGH

LEE

I soon realized that continuously asking "why" was using up a lot of brain-power that I sorely needed for my recovery. There would be a time for asking why, I told myself firmly, but it was not now. Now I needed to focus on getting through each moment as it came.

Even though I hated what was happening with all my being, I finally fully accepted that it had happened. I devoted all my energy and focus to my long and painful rehabilitation. This made the process of recovery truer and more powerful, because I was not distracted by something I had absolutely no control over.

Ecclesiastes 3:4 (NIV), *"There is a time to weep and a time to laugh, a time to mourn and a time to dance."*

By focusing my effort on my recovery, I was

starting to embark on an endeavor that would eventually lead me to an understanding. It was an understanding that when asking God for help with my recovery, I must be willing to do any work necessary and meet God half way.

THE ENDEAVOR

LEE

I still could not move without what seemed like a vomit inducing pain. This was a time when every single part of my consciousness throbbed in bitter anguish, every day and every night.

Jeremiah 23:14 (NIV), *"As for me, I am in your hands; do with me whatever you think is good and right."*

LEE

Felled by pain and weakened to the point of exhaustion, I came to the realization that some sort of intervention was needed if I wanted to be able to overcome and make it through the pain to a full recovery. I was not going to spend the rest of my life needing assistance with simple, everyday activities if I had anything to do with it, so I pleaded for help. I said this silent prayer to myself: "Thank you Lord for what has happened: whatever occurs from here, let it be your will."

JOURNAL

11/15: In an exciting development, Lee sat on the side of his bed for 15 minutes today. He was then helped to his feet by the therapist and walked 15 steps with a walker. He sat in a hospital chair for about an hour.

11/16: Lee seems to look at all of his therapy, be it physical or respiratory, as a personal challenge.

LEE

Things continued to be awful. There was a constant thundering pain in every moment. Day by day, as I began to heal, the daily burn dressings were getting more painful. Therapy seemed to not be helping, it seemed to only cause more pain, and the progression was very slow. Even though I had many folks who were always there for me, I was still in a state of denial. There were moments of sheer confidence accompanied by moments of great sorrow that seemed to plague my hopes for recovery. I was truly on a roller coaster of emotions.

One of my nurses was Melvin, who I first remember coming in to give me a shave. Soon after, I decided to try and grow a beard, which to my amazement I grew. I had always wanted a beard but was never able to grow one. I remember that Melvin saw my beard, he smiled and told me that the way to recovery was within my grasp. He encouraged me to not ever give up. During my darkest hours, I recall Melvin kneeling at the foot of my bed and singing "Amazing Grace" to me as I struggled with my present pain and the pain of my uncertain future.

I will always remember Melvin for the utter compassion he showed me and my family, and for the fortitude he instilled into me by constantly telling me that I could not ever give up.

2 Chronicles 20:17 (NIV), *"You will not have to fight this battle. Take up your positions; stand firm and see the deliverance the Lord will give you, Judah and Jerusalem. Do not be afraid; do not be discouraged. Go out to face them tomorrow, and the Lord will be with you."*

V. TBNU CONTINUED

"Every night of our lives, we dream, and our brain concocts visions which are, at least until we wake up, highly convincing. Most of us have had experiences which are verging on hallucination. It shows the power of the brain to knock up illusions." **Richard Dawkins**

HALLUCINATION

I thought my hospital bed was a small sail boat, and I was going to paddle it from Peru to Australia. I was using a paddle and battling the waves and winds of the Pacific in my sails; up and down I went through the ocean swells, up and down. Through storms and sunny days, I constantly paddled to try and make it to dry land, but I never did. I then woke.

LEE

My good friend and head burn nurse on the floor at the time (G. Burns) was in the room during this hallucination. After I woke up, I found it funny; I had heard stories of people all over the world praying for me. My parents had told me that people were praying for me from the countries of Peru and Australia. G. Burns helped me back to reality by telling me that I was not in a sailboat but a hospital bed, that I was not battling the Pacific Ocean but recovering from being burned.

I had started to have hallucinations and vivid dreams due to two factors: an allergic reaction to some of the pain meds I was being given and from the monotony of being in an ICU environment for many weeks.

My hallucinations became worse. There were times when I would see people in my hospital room and carry on conversations with them.

I would talk about bowling.

"Bowling is a science. There is no one way of doing it properly. However, you must grasp certain fundamentals if you wish to be successful. Of utmost importance is your timing at the foul line when you release the ball."

It appeared to my parents and to visitors that I was out of my mind.

JOURNAL

11/17: Lee will have another swallow test tomorrow. Doctor Cross (head burn doctor) said once he passes the test we can remove the nasal-gastro tube and he can start eating solid food. Today Lee spoke with his manager. The call was reassuring for him, because despite assurances otherwise, Lee has been concerned that his manager still does not know where he is.

11/19: Lee failed his swallow test and cannot yet eat solid foods.

FEAR

Isaiah 43:2 (NIV), *"When you pass through the waters, I will be with you; and when you pass* *through the rivers they will not sweep over you. When you walk through the fire, you will not be burned; the flames will not set you ablaze."*

HALLUCINATION

I was in a gorge, a place surrounded on all sides by sheer mountain cliffs except for a tributary that led to a lake at its center. At the water's edge there was a pier that sat atop the lake. It was a dark, overcast night. I could see the outlined silhouettes of the tops of the trees. Everything was black and white, and there were many sinister boulders in the gorge on dry land, sloping down a small incline connecting to the water. I saw in the distance slowly floating towards me, a Tom Sawyer like-flotilla. On it was a bright and glowing life form.

I panicked and jumped to hide behind one of the many boulders in the gorge. When the glowing object made it to the pier, it just stood and waited. I stayed as still as possible. Finally, it got back on its raft and floated away. As it was leaving, I realized that it was Jesus. I ran onto the pier as the object floated out of sight, but I was too late. I stood and wept.

Shortly after He had floated out of sight, I saw something else floating towards me. It looked similar to what I had just seen, but I was scared that it might be something different, so I hid behind another boulder in the gorge. I was still and waited. In a nightmarish repetition, the scene repeated itself. The object got off its raft and stood on the pier, then left. Again it was Jesus. I ran back onto the pier as He was floating away, and, again, I cried.

TERI, CHURCH FRIEND

One night when I was watching Lee, who had been sleeping very deeply, he opened his eyes and said loudly, "Do you see that?"

I asked, "See what, Lee?" I knew we were the only ones in the room, but he seemed insistent that we were not alone.

Lee said "That!" His voice was getting louder and more convincing.

"Where is it, Lee?"

"There!"

"No, Lee, I don't."

In a sad voice, he replied "Okay." He closed his eyes and a moment later he was back to sleep.

I have always wondered what he saw.

LEE

I was experiencing many doubts about what was happening to me at present and for my future as a whole. I imagined a terrifying future of constant pain and the continued brutality of burn dressings. That thought made me desire with everything I had to become once again completely independent and fully recovered.

THE MOMENT

LEE

During the next few days the great effort continued. Even though I knew the pain and what to expect with daily burn dressings, I still felt that the pain was eating me alive with every single moment. Besides some physical therapy, I was confined to a hospital bed. The skin-ripping agony of daily burn dressings seemed to be multiplying. I had no clear understanding of when or if my wounds would ever heal. I anxiously wondered if I would spend the rest of my days in a constant damning pain. These moments of self-pity started to settle in and I became incredibly depressed about what was happening.

I read a verse from a <u>Bible</u> given to my family by a good friend on the morning of the fire. It sat by my bed, and visitors had underlined specific passages. The verse I recall reading was **John 9: 3 (NIV)**, *"Neither this man nor his parents sinned,"* said Jesus, *"but this happened so that the work of God might be displayed in his life."*

I came to the full realization that it is not what happens to us that defines us; it is what we each do with the situation we are handed that ultimately matters. I decided to make a personal commitment.

This was a personal commitment I made to my

very soul-a commitment that I would get better. I would completely heal or I would spend the rest of my life attempting to do so. I was "all in." I would hold nothing back; no matter how long it took, I would be healed or die trying. I could care less what others thought or said. I would go at my own pace and do my very best to make sure I fully recovered.

To myself I said this prayerful commitment: "God, thank you for what you have done. All I ask is that you give me the strength, the will, and the determination to endure this time in my life. Although I do not understand why this is happening to me, I do acknowledge that it is beyond my understanding and that I need You to help me. I will work through the pain and all of the restrictions. Amen."

"You cannot control what happens to you, but you can control your attitude toward what happens to you, and in that, you will be mastering change rather than allowing it to master you."
Brian Tracy

A REMEMBRANCE

HALLUCINATION

I was in the Cosby show; I was the neighbor. The crowd cheered as I walked into the Huxtable home to see Doctor Cosby. Doctor Cosby and I sat on his couch and talked about being burned and my other worries.

LEE

I woke up with a laugh from my hallucination. The Cosby show was frequently on in my room. One of my good friends, Doctor Banks, who was my Sunday school teacher and one who visited me often, is a gynecologist. This was the role Doctor Cosby played on his show. Visitors and television, my old and new lives, were conflicting and becoming distorted in my dreams. I did not know what was real and what was not, but it still made me laugh.

JOURNAL

11/21: Physical therapy had Lee standing up for 10 minutes, and then he walked down the hallway about 45 feet with a walker. He sat in his chair for about an hour. I could tell it was painful and scary at times, but April and I could see the determination in his eyes and on his face.

"I prayed for twenty years but received no answer until I prayed with my legs." **Frederick Douglas**

LEE

After being placed back into bed, my body raged in pain, but now I remembered. I remembered what it felt like to stand and to walk. I remember what it felt like to bowl, what it felt like to drive, what it felt like to cook outside, what it felt like to play a game of chess. I remembered what it was like to be completely pain-free.

This was my ultimate goal, my vision: to be

as pain-free and as independent as I once was, as in my memories. I remembered that it will feel better when it quits hurting. I was able to start to envision a recovery. The realization also brought a greater understanding of the gap between where I had been and where I was now. It brought a greater understanding of the severity of my burns and an acceptance of what it would take to recover.

I started to look at things very differently. I embraced what had occurred by facing it rather than trying to run away and deny it. With a very clear realization of the ensuing struggle, I had enlightening thoughts of what it would take to become rehabilitated. The time had come to hold nothing back. The time had come to push forward with an undying effort. This is when I learned to meet God half-way. This was the moment when my recovery truly began, and when my faith was solidified.

This restored faith was different from the faith I had before the fire. This was a faith in which I knew that if the Lord gave me the strength, regardless of the outcome or how long it took, I would continue to make a recovery. This was a faith in which I knew my family and friends would always be there for me. This was a simple faith in which I knew that as long as I held up my side of the personal commitment, I would not only make the effort to recover, but ultimately use the experience to help others learn something amazing.

"Life is a storm. You will bask in the sunlight one moment, be shattered on the rocks the next. What makes you a man is what you do when that storm comes. You must look into that storm and shout, "Do your worst, for I will do mine!""
Alexandre Dumas

With this realization and renewed faith came a deep heartfelt desire to recover, a desire to become completely rehabilitated. Without the awareness of what had occurred, I would not have been able to face the reality of what was happening.

FOOD

JOURNAL

11/22: Lee was weighed today and he is at 137 pounds. He weighed 176 pounds upon admittance to the ER. They will redo the swallow test Thursday or Friday. Therapy continues with walking and standing.

11/23: Lee's medical team continue to mention how polite he is and that he has been wishing everyone a Happy Thanksgiving. Today marks 39 days in the hospital.

LEE

The next day was Thanksgiving, which fell on my dad's birthday. On this day, I finally passed a test to begin eating solid food. The date was November 24, 2005. Time in the hospital was 40 days.

JOURNAL

11/24: Lee called to say he has passed his swallow test. He immediately requested turkey and green beans prepared by his Nana, Milo's brand sweet tea and Dr. Pepper. Today is David's birthday. Today Lee was visited by many family members, including Beecher O. from church, whose birthday is also today.

LEE

My mouth was larger than my stomach. It was fantastic to eat solid food again but I was filled up quickly because my stomach had shrunk due to 40 days without solid food and limited physical activity.

JOURNAL

11/24: Lee has been having muscle spasms in his arms and legs several times a day, but today they were much worse. When the spasm hits, he jerks his arm/and or leg, which causes intense pain. Doctor Cross says this is normal for burn patients.

11/26: Lee has been hallucinating from lack of sleep and a possible allergic reaction to medication. David helped Lee walk 60 feet with a walker today.

LEE

My unrelenting muscle spasms extended my arms and legs more than I had extended them in therapy, which added to the jerking pain. One morning, I yelled at my brother, Brian, when he walked past the foot of my bed at the same time that I had one of these violent twitches in my leg.

On multiple occasions, my mom and my sister-in-law, April, had to stand over my bed and hold me down due to the violent seizure-like twitches.

My right arm seemed to have grown a mind of its own. It would involuntarily rise into a position as if I were holding up my hand to ask a question. I had no control over the arm. Someone would lower my arm to my side, but it would slowly rise again as far as it physically could.

Daily burn dressings continued. My hallucinations were getting more intense.

One time, as I came in and out of a feverish hallucination, my mother sat next to my bed singing a song into my ear. "Jesus, Jesus, Jesus, there's just something about that name." This took place before a dreaded torture session that was in the form of a burn dressing.

Nurses would always pump more pain meds into me before one of these chamber times, but there were never enough meds to take the pain away. During this specific burn dressing, I was having another hallucinatory reaction to the pain meds. These hallucinations were different than any other dream I had ever had before. I could feel physical pain during them, which is something that I have never experienced in any dream.

HALLUCINATION

I was in a distant land with my mom and a small group of people. I had begun to feel the pain from the removal of my bandages and the cleaning of my wounds through the foggy haze. Suddenly, the lyrics "Jesus, Jesus, Jesus, there's just something about the name," began to wind through my head on repeat. The pain went away completely. I felt nothing as long as that song was playing in my head.

LEE

The next day I recalled a time of no pain. I tried desperately to remember the song, but could not. The dressing change that day was a fiendish, tormenting pain. I plunged into the depths of a new hallucinatory reaction. I wandered through the dark haze of my dreams with a feeling of great sorrow.

After the most recent and very painful burn dressing, I asked Mom about that Russian song. She replied that she did not know of any Russian song and thought that I was once again out of my mind. There had been something about Russia on the news at the time, and the news stories twisted in and out of my thoughts, confusing me.

It grew into an obsession; all I thought

about was the song. After several days and many attempts to explain it to confused family members, I was finally able to hum the tune and was reminded of the words. Hearing it again, the pain briefly ceased. This was the first time since the fire that I felt no pain.

In my experience, pain meds just distract your brain from focusing on the pain. "Jesus, Jesus, Jesus, there's just something about that name" is a song that I relied upon when I was in great pain. I was on a large dosage of pain meds that just dulled the pain and made it tolerable, but this song provided my mind with enough dissent to completely take away the pain away for the first time. "Jesus, Jesus, Jesus, there's just something about that name" is a song that delivered me when I was at my weakest. This was a victory in Jesus.

Acts 2: 21(NIV), *"And whoever calls on the name of the Lord will be saved."*

JOURNAL

11/27: I saw most of Lee's burned areas today. His stomach and chest look better than they did when I last saw them. I cannot comprehend how much this must hurt. Lee asked what was the name of that "Russian song" I sang to him (which was probably a hallucination). He started humming the tune and the song was "Jesus, Jesus, Jesus, there's just something about that name." Lee is still having some major muscle spasms and body jerks with some times of confusion. We've been told this is probably due to 43 days in an ICU environment and sleep deprivation. Melvin came by and sang "Amazing Grace."

DR. PEPPER

HALLUCINATION

I was sitting in a wheelchair in a long, skinny hallway. I heard a voice in my head say "Stand up and walk, you lazy jackass." I gathered my strength, stood up, and walked without any pain or any restriction, no doubt or fear. This was the last time I was pain free until my wounds finally closed.

Luke 17:19 (NIV), *"Then he said to me. Rise and go; your faith has made you well."*

LEE

Once I awoke I knew for certain I would eventually be fully recovered.

JOURNAL

11/28: A psychiatrist has been called to evaluate Lee. He is almost certain that these hallucinations are being caused by meds and sleep deprivation.

11/29: Lee's meds were changed. His hallucinations and muscle spasms have stopped, and he slept for six hours. Doctor Cross discussed his next skin graft and mentioned that skin grafts seem to take very well to Lee's body.

LEE S.

Lee wanted a Dr. Pepper. After all of the hours, the days, the weeks of praying, all my brother Lee wanted was a Dr. Pepper. He didn't talk much, and whenever he did, I had no idea what we would speak about. I knew that he was in pain and I did not want to upset him more. I just wanted my friend to know I was there for him.

12/1: Doctor Cross came to speak with Lee about his next surgery. Lee's only question was, "Will you put me to sleep?" Lee does not recall any previous talk or experiences of skin graft surgeries. Doctor Cross is pleased with Lee's progress and he wants him to get out of bed and do more therapy. There have been no more shakes or hallucinations. Lee's medical team continues to be in awe of his politeness.

JOURNAL

12/4: Talked with head burn nurse, G. Burns, who told me there is no medical explanation for Lee's ability to breathe normally with the carbon monoxide level accompanied by his lung inhalation injury.

12/5: Lee has been in a good amount of pain this afternoon that took awhile to get under control. Through it all, he doesn't want to complain.

12/6: Lee's Uncle Roger came by and seemed impressed by his beard. One of Uncle Roger's pastors came by to visit this afternoon and prayed. I smiled when Lee started snoring during the prayer. Lee seemed to have a lot of anxiety at the sight of the burn dressing team today. This team has changed his dressings since day one. Lee gets moved onto his side frequently to get him off of his buttocks. Tonight when his Aunt Patty asked him which direction he wanted to be faced, he said "Home."

THE BROTHERHOOD

JOURNAL

12/5/2006: Today Lee was visited by a member of the Burn Survivor team at UAB. This is a special team of burn survivors whose job is to encourage, lift up, and answer questions for other burn survivors and their families. This member's name is Dave.

I first met Dave while Lee was in the ICU. He came and stood by Lee's nurse and introduced himself to David and me. He said, "My name is Dave. I was burned on 85% of my body. I am a survivor! Lee will be too!" Then, he gave me a big hug.

LEE

I had my first visit that I remember from a burn survivor. He asked if I had any questions for him about being burned. I tried to explain the type of pain I was experiencing, and he said he knew exactly what I was talking about. Somehow, this was a relief. I knew I was not alone in my overbearing pain and was happy to speak with someone who had experienced the same Hell.

He then told me about the "burn tank," which is how they used to do burn dressing changes. The patient's dressings were clipped off, then he or she would be submerged into water into a bath tub that resembled a large fish tank. The patient's wounds would be scrubbed with brushes, dried off, and bandaged up.

I asked G. Burns later if this was truly how burn dressing changes used to be performed, and he confirmed. I was extremely thankful that this burn survivor took the time to truthfully speak with me and especially grateful that this was not how a burn dressing was performed today.

From then on, I remember frequent visits by members of the burn survivor team.

"We don't even know how strong we are until we are forced to bring that hidden strength forward. In times of tragedy, of war, of necessity, people do amazing things. The human

capacity for survival and renewal is awesome."
Isabel Allende

DAVID LUCAS

What a character! During his visit, Dave asked if we had any questions for him. He started to explain how donor skin was taken from his waist and buttocks and used for skin grafts to cover open wounds on the top his head. He invited me to touch the top of his head to feel how a healed graft felt. So, I did. He then said, "Now you know how my butt feels."

TERI

Every time I left after visiting Lee, I would say "Cowboy up." Others might consider this insensitive, but Lee seemed to take it as a call to push forward. For me, it meant that I knew Lee could do whatever it takes to make it through his ordeal and become completely rehabilitated.

JOURNAL

12/8: Lee walked 56 feet today with a walker.

12/10: Lee walked 90 feet with a walker today. Weight is 126 pounds. I asked Lee if he needed anything. He said a ride home.

LEE

I wanted to go home. I was sick and tired of being in the hospital and wanted to return to my life as I remembered it.

I received a call from bowling buddy, Dan R., who said that they were waiting to destroy me in bowling. I replied that he was lucky I was in the hospital.

T-BONE

JOURNAL

12/16: When Doctor Cross speaks on our floor, the medical team jumps. One of the visitors asked him if Lee would be transferred to another doctor for rehab. His response was, "I do not transfer my patients to anyone."

DAVE

George and I slow cooked a very large T-bone steak and rushed it to Lee as soon as we took it off the grill.

GEORGE

Dave bought a fat T-bone steak and brought it to my apartment along with a small charcoal grill. We slow cooked it to take to Lee. It took awhile, but when the steak was finished and Dave was removing it from the grill, the meat came right off the bone. This steak was cooked through and very tender. Dave wrapped it in foil and brought it to Lee to devour.

JOURNAL

12/17: Tim and Jeanne H., parents of Lee's long time childhood friend, Carter, came and visited today. Bowling buddies George and Dave brought Lee a huge T-bone steak. Michael H. and Jeff W., from Lee's Sunday school class, stopped by and gave Lee a movie. G. Burns came by to say that Lee was telling jokes and had everyone laughing during his dressing change today.

LEE

Ashley H., Tim and Jeanne's daughter and friend Carter's sister, called and told me that she thought I was very brave. I considered this. I felt I had no other choice. I had to go through this regardless of how I felt about it. She said she knew of many people who would not be able to handle the injury as I had, and she just wanted to tell me how brave I was. I said, "Thank you."

As I hung up, I thought, no one knows what he can handle until he goes through it. I still had a long way to go to recovery. I must not give up.

I watched the movie given to me by Sunday school class friends, the new "Starsky and Hutch," which I had not yet seen.

JOURNAL

12/18: This morning Melvin, Lee's nurse, came and asked if Lee would talk with another burn patient that was in his same unit. Lee agreed. He told this person that he was in the very best place for recovery, not only because of the care, but also due to the fact that the nurses would never let him give up hope. However, he would have to fully commit with his mind, body and soul to work through his recovery. Melvin bragged around the hallway about Lee's willingness to speak with and comfort another burn survivor.

LEE

I heard later that this fellow burn patient I spoke to had made a full recovery.

Marge, a burn dressing team member, was very surprised when I preferred to stand instead of lying on the table during my dressing change.

On December 19, 2005, Doctor Cross released me from his care. I was off to Spain Rehabilitation Center at UAB, where my therapy would become more intense and my burn dressings would be cut to every other day. I would begin recreational therapy as a final measure to determine if I had an anoxic brain injury. I would resume occupational and physical therapy. I was fine with not having a burn dressing every day and with pressing forward in the new therapy needed to get me home and back to work. Doctor Bagley would become my doctor. I would be visited by Doctor Cross once a week to check my progress. This was my 65th day in the hospital, and my good friend Dave's birthday.

G. BURNS, BURN CHARGE NURSE

One of the most notable things about Lee's stay was that he was never without a family member, church member, or friend at his bedside. They were all present, praying, and supporting him, and this was the thing that kept him improving and making progress far faster than anyone I had seen in my time on that unit.

VI. Spain Rehab

JOURNAL

12/20: At Spain Rehab Center, Lee was swarmed upon admission by the people who work in the unit. They had apparently heard of him. Dressing changes are getting more painful as nerve the endings grow back. Dave and George, two of Lee's bowling buddies, came by to visit. Lee was told that a collection was taken for Lee at the bowling alley to fund the remainder of his bowling league, which runs from September to May and charges a weekly fee. It has been decided that a central line will be put back into Lee for more blood transfusions.

12/21: Lee went to rehab today. It was tough and painful, but Lee kept at it.

LEE

After my rehab exercises, I had an ice-cold lemon-lime flavored Gatorade. I gulped it down through a straw as though it was the first beverage I had had in years. It was the most physically refreshing supplement I have ever had.

THE RULE

1 Timothy 4:16 (NIV), *"Watch your life and doctrine closely. Persevere in them, because if you do, you will save yourself and your hearers."*

LEE

"Don't give up Lee," raced through my head on repeat, "I don't care if it hurts. I will walk farther than they ask me to. I will employ my 118% rule."

This rule is based on the element of time, with 100% being an hour (60 minutes). Thus 118% would be 70 minutes on a 60 minute scale.

I would do 118% of everything the therapist requested. To accomplish this, I would relate my therapy to a great personal struggle as I had before. I would break down each task to its most common denominator, then repeat.

The common denominators that were present were the physical, mental and attitudinal aspects of recovery.

The physical aspect was going through the pain and horror of burn dressings and the seemingly never ending sting of physical therapy while having open wounds over the majority of my body.

The mental aspect was made up of emotions. One's mental state determines their motivation to move forward or not. I would use those emotions to my advantage during my recovery. I would turn these emotions upside down to make my recovery a reality. How I viewed what I was going through helped me to determine the mental aspect of my recovery.

The attitudinal aspect was the most important of the three. Attitude encompasses not only the mental and physical, but also expectations and the planning of what comes next. Attitude was the most difficult, because it required the seemingly unthinkable. Attitude required that I accepted what had happened and keep moving on.

Attitude reflects ownership and can therefore work wonders beyond a person's imagination. But it can also destroy all that is around us if not maintained by continuously acknowledging that it is our responsibility to work through recovery.

By breaking each task down and fitting it into one or more of these categories, I was able to place more focus on my recovery. I was able to easily distinguish in my head a clear view of each specific task. The simplicity of my understanding made the process of repeating each task very easy.

JOURNAL

12/23: I arrived at Spain Rehab Center about halfway through Lee's therapy. Papa saw Lee walk 170 feet with a walker after the therapist set an initial goal of 100 feet. He walked more after some knee and ankle stretches. Lee mentioned that he was having pain in his right heel.

LEE

All I have to do is walk more than my therapist asks, and I have to do it 500 times. I must rebuild my muscle memory one step at a time. I must regain the ability to walk without thinking about it, I thought.

CHRISTMAS

JOURNAL

12/24: Lee was visited by Aunt Patty and Bailey, a black lab therapy dog from a group Patty volunteers with. The group sends these specially trained dogs to visit with patients who are rehabilitating from traumatic injuries. Lee's whole countenance changed when the therapy dog, Bailey, laid his head on Lee's bed. He mentioned that his right heel continued to hurt.

LEE

At 7 p.m., I switched the TV to watch "A Christmas Story," which had a 24-hour run. I did not change the channel for the next 24 hours. Those who were there with me did not appreciate it, but I found it hilarious.

JOURNAL

12/25: Lee started Christmas morning with Brian, April and the girls, and David and me. Lee had many visitors, from childhood friends to church friends to family. We were not going to spend Christmas without our son Lee if we could help it. It was a special time.

LEE

I was visited by my five-and almost-two-year old nieces, Claudia and Julia, along with Brian and April. George and Dave also came and visited. I was thankful for the visits on Christmas day but upset that I would not be able to join in the fun of being there on Christmas morning as my nieces opened their gifts. Dave and George made a surprise, and I was happy to see them and very thankful for their visit.

GEORGE

During our visit on Christmas day, Mrs. Lucas asked me to pose for a picture with Lee because we both had beards. I have that picture on my mirror so I can see it every day. It reminds me of what Lee went through and how he persevered. It reminds me that no matter what challenges present themselves, I need to keep a true attitude, have confidence in myself, and keep my focus on the goals I want to achieve.

12/26: Lee and David had a decent night. They played Battleship to prepare for recreational therapy. Speaking with them, of course, I cannot tell who won.

CHESS

JOURNAL

12/27: Lee's right foot and heel are still causing great pain in therapy. This may be from a wound he has on his right heel. The doctor should be here tomorrow and hopefully we can have some aggressive interrogation as to why he is having this pain.

12/28: An X-ray of Lee's right foot revealed a hairline fracture on the bone that goes to the little toe on top of the foot. The doctor is going to provide Lee with a special shoe for support to keep the pressure off that part of the foot. We just hope this shoe will help him to be able to walk more. Lee's heart rate and pain level were up today, but he ate as if he had not eaten in ages. Lee is pushing his recovery like no other I have ever seen.

LEE

Recreational therapy consisted of playing games designed to restore, remediate and rehabilitate a person's level of functioning and independence in life activities according to my therapist. We played the card game Rummy, Checkers, Boggle, Sudoku and put jigsaw puzzles together. I asked if there was a chess board. To my surprise one was not available. All over UAB? No chess board? I asked if we could get one.

JOURNAL

12/30: The doctor and rehab people put together a shoe to help relieve the pressure on Lee's foot, something that will make it less painful to walk. Lee's cousin, Matt, went with him to therapy today. He did mainly upper-body exercises. The burn dressing team leader, Karen, said Lee's wounds and grafts are healing very well, and there is no infection. Lee's right foot is really swollen tonight. Lee's case continues to amaze his medical team. His nurse told me this afternoon that she had read his file from the morning he was admitted. I took the opportunity to share with her the healing the Lord had done.

JASON, CHILDHOOD FRIEND

Lee and I work for the same company. We've taken up a collection of things for Lee due to the fact he had lost most all his possessions. One thing I got him was a new pair of shoes. Sherice and I delivered them to Lee along with some UNO cards for recreational therapy.

LEE

I assumed that everything I owned in my condo was damaged or completely destroyed. At that point, I had no knowledge of anything that survived the fire. I was worried about a Mickey Mantle autographed picture I had but was almost certain was destroyed. However, I had put it out of my mind. It was not as important as my recovery.

JOURNAL

12/31: Lee's buddies Dave, George and John, brought him a chess board today. Jason and his girlfriend Sherice brought him some UNO cards.

JOURNAL

1/4/2006: Therapy went very well today. Lee's new shoe appears to be relieving the pain from his fractured toe while walking. Lee's buddies John, George, and Dave, came by before bowling tonight. Doctor Oleson, one of Lee's therapy doctors, said she worked the burn unit for the Pentagon after 9/11. Burns are her secondary specialty.

JOURNAL

1/7/2006: Lee's heel appears to be healing. It does not hurt as much, and he is elated that he can walk more in therapy now.

1/8/2006: Lee's therapists asked if he was ready to walk 100 feet today. Lee said "Let's do it," then walked 150 feet with a walker. Lee beat his chess buddy, John, in a game of chess today.

JOHN

The chess game in the hospital was good. Lee had made some bad moves at the start. I was up by two major pieces, a knight and a bishop, but I was down three pawns to two. I started to work on my fortifications. Before I knew it, Lee was up on me by two pieces. And then he won. Our past games had typically been decided by the one who made the first mistake. It was good to see Lee's mind working as well as it had in the past.

LEE

I asked John later if he had allowed me to win. He said he had not. He said he backed off when he gained the greater advantage to build up his base.

"You shouldn't have done that," I said.

I took the chess board and all 32 pieces to therapy and donated it to the stack of games that were available for recreational therapy.

2 Corinthians 8:2-3 (NIV), *"In the midst of a very severe trial, their overflowing joy and their extreme poverty welled up in rich generosity. For I testify they gave as much as they were able, and even beyond their ability."*

HOT DOG

LEE

Lee, don't you ever give up on me raced through my head as I walked. *Do not ever give up.*

JOURNAL

1/9/2006: Lee told me he walked 200 feet today with his walker and was able to stand unassisted for six to eight minutes.

LEE

Dammit Lee, you stupid dumb-ass. Do not ever give up on me, I repeated over and over.

JOURNAL

1/10/2006: Lee's doctor said that he is making great progress and her goal for him is to walk 150 feet each therapy session for the time being. Lee's sister-in-law, April, was with him in therapy as he walked 400 feet with a walker. He then rested and walked another 300 feet. Lee also stood for several minutes unassisted. After therapy, Lee asked for a hot dog with mustard, relish and onions.

LEE S.

I remember chess and Lee. I heard from his nurse, who was bragging about how much progress Lee had made while maintaining a healthy attitude for recovery. I heard her say that Lee was telling jokes during his walking therapy.

Previously, I had hoped Lee would make it. Now, after witnessing his progress, I knew he would.

GOING OUTSIDE

JOURNAL

1/11/2006: Nana and Papa were so excited to see Lee walk 475 feet with a walker today. Lee's bone scan came back this afternoon. His fracture is healing well. Lee asked why I have to brag to everyone I see about his walking. I told him I'll never be able to be quiet about how well he is doing. I can vividly remember 10/16/2005 and what little hope he was given.

Lee told me not to dwell on the past. "It's over; we'll revisit it at another time. Instead, let's focus on getting out of here."

GRANDPARENTS PAPA & NAPA

Therapy, though painful for Lee, was a most welcome event. We were able to relieve David and Anne to some extent by accompanying Lee to his therapy sessions at UAB. We were pleased that we could help, so we spent many days with Lee as he participated in the exercises which would help him prepare for a return to life after his tragic accident.

JOURNAL

1/12/2006: This morning Doctor Oleson, one of the rehab doctors, told Lee that therapy next week would include climbing stairs and pivoting on one foot. In recreational therapy, they had Lee playing Boggle. I understand that John wants a chess rematch after he lost to Lee. Lee walked 610 feet total with his walker today. Afterward, David wheeled Lee outside to the patio, where it was an unseasonably warm temperature of 70 degrees. This is the first time Lee has been outside since the accident.

LEE

It was nice to be outside again. Even though I was in a wheelchair, my brief time outdoors, taking in the seemingly fresh city air was something that encouraged me to get home.

JOURNAL

1/13/2006: Walking with a walker is getting easier for Lee. He climbed three steps today, which was his first time walking up an incline.

JOURNAL

1/15/2006: Aunt Dale and Uncle Darell were with Lee during physical therapy today. Lee walked 440 feet today. He acts as if these distances are no big deal, though we can see how difficult they are. The burn dressing team came to Spain rehab to do the dressing change. Lee was in more pain than usual due to his nerve endings growing back, but he takes it with unbelievable patience and very few cries of pain.

JOURNAL

1/16/2006: Although Lee had extra pain in his knees and hips, he walked 450 feet today and spent time stepping up onto a small box that was the size of a step. Retired pediatrician Doctor Money, a church friend, stopped by and seemed pleased at Lee's progress. Lee and Connie B. from church also stopped by and saw Lee with his beard. They said that he looked different these days.

JOURNAL

1/17/2006: Lee beat one of his therapists at chess today during recreational therapy. Then, he and Papa played poker. David arrived in time to accompany Lee as he walked 750 feet with a walker.

JOURNAL

1/18/2006: Today we were asked by the burn dressing team to wrap Lee's gauze with an ace bandage while they observed. This was in order to prepare for his return home. Lee got out of bed and balanced himself standing while holding onto a chair. Then he gave us orders on what to do, and how to do it. Ace bandages are used so that the gauze does not move around too much during therapy. Today, Lee walked 700 feet with his walker. Then, he stood for 20 minutes, keeping his left foot on a step-level box for 10 minutes, then switching feet for the remaining 10 while he worked a puzzle. Mike, Dave, George, and John came by before bowling tonight.

JOURNAL

1/20/2006: Lee and April played a mind logic game today. Then, Lee walked 800 feet with his walker and stood 14 minutes while working a puzzle. Lee was visited by our former pastor, Brother Jim and his wife Oleta, today. Lee said he felt bad for not talking more while they were there. Today the burn dressing team came by the Spain rehab room and asked us to change his dressings. We cut off his bandages which are from his mid-chest to his ankles. I took my time because I did not want to hurt him. Lee then helped us use the portable shower-head to rinse the wounds. He explained, in great detail, how to soap up a washcloth and gently clean the wounds, then rinse and dab them with a dry towel. Lee helped rinse his body again. The burn dressing team was there to bandage him up afterwards.

JOURNAL

1/21/2006: Lee walked 950 feet with his walker today and beat his dad at three games of chess. He stood for 25 minutes while playing a board game. Lee and I talked about his wounds today. Lee does not dwell on what happened or why he is made to go through this. His concentration is on what he needs to do in therapy and getting back to work. Lee's friends Dave, George, and John, stopped by with some grilled bratwurst. Then some more friends, Mike, Jennifer, Jody and Jill, stopped by for a visit.

ENCOURAGEMENT

GEORGE

Mr. Lucas asked me to install a hardwood floor in the room where Lee would stay at their house. I worked for my father's tile company at the time. Since I've never installed a hardwood floor, I asked John to help. Despite our lack of experience installing hardwood floors, Mr. Lucas was sure we were the ones for the job.

JOURNAL

1/22/2006: In therapy, Lee concentrated on stretches which are critical for burn survivors to keep the joints flexible. He climbed four steps and went down them backwards, then decided on his own to walk with his walker. Lee walked 700 feet. This afternoon while Lee slept, I read a book given to me by one of Lee's doctor's called "Refined by Fire." The book is about a man named Lieutenant Colonel Birdwell who was severely burned while working in the Pentagon on 9/11. Reading this book maintained my hope for Lee's recovery through our Lord Jesus Christ. Lee is doing well, swinging his feet off the bed, standing, then getting into a seated position, which looks very painful. Russell M., a good friend, retrofitted our downstairs bathroom to accommodate Lee. He will need hand rails in the shower, by the sink and toilet.

JOURNAL

1/23/2006: Today marks 100 days in the hospital. Doctors Oleson and Bagley stopped by to say they think Lee can go home a week from today. When asked what Lee thought about that he said, "Great. Let's do it! Less talk, more do." Lee got out of bed without any assistance today. During therapy, he climbed eight steps.

JOURNAL

1/24/2006: In therapy today, Lee was made to do several stretches, one in which he used a six-foot ladder. He bent over and took cones from the bottom rung of the ladder and stacked them, one by one, on the top rung. Bailey, the black lab therapy dog, visited Lee and the rest of the patients in therapy today. All the patients at Spain Rehab were excited to see him wagging his tail and greeting everyone.

JOURNAL

1/25/2006: George, John, Mike, and Dave came by before bowling to talk about the Professional Bowling Association tournament that was to occur this weekend in Birmingham. Lee and his dad walked, with his walker, up an incline between Spain Rehab and the hospital to prepare him for the incline into our back door at home. Doctors and nurses are still in awe of the amount of support we have had from family and friends. The whole unit is abuzz at Lee's potential discharge date of 1/30.

JOURNAL

1/26/2006: David drove Lee's truck to the front door of Spain Rehab. Using the handle on the passenger door frame, Lee got into his truck by himself. During therapy, Lee focused on stretching, then went for a walk with his walker.

JOURNAL

1/27/2006: Tonight Lee received a call from Lieutenant General Ron Burgess to check on his progress. He is Deputy Director at the Department of National Intelligence. We know his family from church. You should have heard Lee's voice perk up when he discovered who was on the other end of the line. He also received a personal note from Alabama Governor Bob Riley, who was a Sunday school student of my parents.

LIEUTENANT GENERAL
RON BURGESS (RET)

My wife, Marta had told me about a young man from her home church that had suffered serious burns in an apartment fire.

Lee Lucas had been on our prayer list since we first heard of the accident.

I understood that recovery was going very slowly with a lot of pain. It was not known how long that would go on. One day during my quiet time praying, I felt I should do more for Lee than just pray so I reached out to be an encouragement.

LEE

I received a phone call from General Burgess asking if there was anything he could do for me in Washington. I could not believe who I was talking to. I asked him to say hi to the president for me. I hung up, stunned that this guy took time from his extremely busy job to call and check on me. What a special treat it was. If there was ever anything that was solidly motivating, it was this call.

LIEUTENANT GENERAL
RON BURGESS (RET)

I do not know why I reached out to Lee, but I strongly believed I was led to do it. I think he was a little surprised, given my job, that I would take the time to do that. I tried to explain that there were a lot of believers all over the world praying for him as we were supposed to do. Lee and I agreed to pray for and be an encouragement to each other.

Joshua 1:9 (NIV) *"Have I not commanded you? Be strong and courageous. Do not be afraid, for the Lord your God will be with you wherever you go."*

Today was my mother's birthday.

JOURNAL

1/29/2006: Doctor Bagley came by and asked if Lee was sure he wanted to go home. Lee replied resolutely, "Yes." Therapy was cut short at Lee's request so he could watch the end of the bowling tournament on TV.

JOURNAL

1/30/2006: Day 107.The burn dressing team stopped by Lee's room to change his dressings this morning. They are the same team that has changed his dressings since day one. At 10:45 a.m., Lee made his way to the front door in his wheelchair to go home in his dad's truck. As we rolled onto our street, we saw yellow ribbons everywhere. As we pulled up to the house, we saw many people standing outside cheering. Lee made it up our incline outside and into a recliner in our den. Among the people, there were Lee's nieces, Claudia and Julia, who were so very excited to see their Uncle Lee-Lee. After everyone left, Lee wanted to see the things that had survived the fire. I was not sure what to expect, but he kept insisting, so we did it anyway. He took it well. Lee weighed in at 123 pounds upon release from the hospital.

LEE

Throughout my time in the hospital, there was an enormous effort by friends and family to always make sure I had someone with me, to make sure I had nourishing food and comfort, and to tell me how in the long run God would utilize what happened to me.

When we pulled up to the house, I was astounded by the number of people who were there to greet me. I was happy to see everyone, but anxious to be in a home type-setting again. I was surprised at what possessions had survived the fire. I had not asked too many questions about it and assumed most everything was destroyed. I was grateful that my grandfather's World War II Bible and the Japanese diary he found had survived.

VII. Home

JOURNAL

1/31/2006: Home Health came today to admit Lee into their system. Lee's buddy Carter stopped by before the home health nurse arrived. Carter and I watched as she asked Lee many questions about his pain and well being. When David came home, he had many books about World War II that had been given to him for Lee from the veterans at our church.

LEE

This home health lady asked me each question three separate ways. There was a point when I wanted to scream at her to shut up. I guess there was a reason for her antics.

I was elated that the veterans of my church had donated reading material to me. I was grateful to have such loving support from those who had faced a dire struggle and had made it through on top. I was and will always be forever grateful.

JOURNAL

2/1/2006: The time had come for the first burn dressing at home. A card table had been set up in the den for the supplies. The first step was the clipping off of the bandages, then the shower, and then the re-bandaging of the wounds. Cutting off the bandages was tricky. The home health nurse and I did not want to hurt him, but the bandages were sticking to his wounds, causing great pain for Lee. The home health nurse took pictures of Lee's wounds. Lee rinsed himself in the shower. He gave us specific instructions on the washing of his wounds with Dial soap. After he had rinsed and dried off, Lee came out to be bandaged. It was a tedious task because the bandaging of the wounds took a long while. Afterwards, Lee went to lie down and was quickly asleep.

LEE

My first dressing change at home took more than fifty minutes. I had chairs and walls I could lean against to hold me up, but my legs were so weak that I felt I would collapse onto the floor with open wounds over the majority of my body. I recall thinking that there must be a better way to do this. The way this dressing change was just performed would not work. If these dressing changes were to be done with my mom and dad acting as the nurses, we had to find a more efficient way.

AN UNDERSTANDING

JOURNAL

2/2/2006, Lee climbed seven steps to our kitchen today.

LEE

I remember seeing everyone else walking and climbing steps pain-free. I saw my nieces running and playing without a care in the world. Being pain-free was something I missed. I was longing for a time of no pain and complete independence.

Whenever I stayed in one place for a long time, it became harder to move. My muscles felt heavy, as if they were turning to cement because I had stayed dormant for so long. Nerve endings were growing back, which made the pain of the burns unlike any horror I had ever experienced until that point.

The pain at home was worse than any before. There was another factor that made it worse: I was the only one who was hurt at home. In the hospital I was surrounded by hurting people. Here it was only me.

That night, I lay in bed with my eyes closed. I placed my right index finger onto my left forearm and a light bulb went off in my head. My eyes were closed, but I knew my right index finger had touched my left forearm because my brain said it did. The brain interprets the language of our nerves and tells us what physical state we are in. Since our physical nerves are interpreted by the brain to help the pain, I would need to focus my brain on getting through it rather than dwelling on what pain I was feeling. Because I know it'll feel better when it quits hurting.

JOURNAL

2/3/2006: David helped Lee out of his chair and asked how far he could walk without any assistance. Lee took several steps unassisted. Lee had his second burn dressing at home today. His wounds continue to seep fluid.

LEE

I made it a point to have all the necessary burn supplies, plus 18%, laid out onto the card table before any bandages were clipped off. The bandages were sticking more to my wounds and it felt as if someone was ripping my skin off. But the dressing change did flow much better than the last. Today I was visited by my friend, Quentin, and it was his birthday.

JOURNAL

2/4/2006: Lee's buddy, John, came by and brought him a Civil War chess set. John stayed for a while, but they didn't play chess. I think he wanted a re-match, but Lee was more fatigued today than usual.

LEE

During our third burn dressing, all the supplies were set up before we clipped any bandages. The home health nurse was not there, so my parents would be performing the dressing change. I had decided to time the process so I would know exactly what progress was being made. Today's dressing change took less than 40 minutes.

LEE S.

It was great to see Lee out of a hospital setting, but it also made me realize how much healing lay ahead of him. It seemed daunting. It was painful to watch him move; I could see how much it hurt him and it hurt me. I was tired of my friend suffering.

JOURNAL

2/8/2006: Lee's bowling buddies came to visit before bowling tonight. They talked about when Lee would make a visit to the bowling alley.

THE SPLENDID SPLINTER

JOURNAL

2/9/2006: Lee saw Doctor Cross today and had a burn dressing at UAB. He was in and out within an hour with a report that the wounds are healing nicely. Sandy B., one of Lee's Sunday school teachers, brought Lee a book about healing through humor. According to Lee, the dressing change today took 38 minutes. David drove Lee by his burned condo today. Lee's Uncle Darell gave him a whole processed and packaged deer he had shot. Lee has been ordered to eat a lot of red meat to bring up his blood count.

LEE

The outside of my condo looked as it had in the photos that I was shown a few months before, but was much different in person. The burnt structure looked horrifying and damning. I wondered how I could have been rescued from that condo after seeing how it looked in person.

The firemen who rescued me deserved more than I could ever give them.

JOURNAL

2/11/2006: Lee was making a list of things he had lost in his condo while I was upstairs working. I heard a thump, went downstairs, and saw Lee on the floor thrashing his arms. I helped him back up, and asked what happened. He said he needed to get something that required him to stand up and walk, and that was when he fell. I asked why he didn't call me. He said, laughing, that he did not want to bug me.

LEE

I thought, *I can stand and walk*. I pushed with my arms on my wheelchair handle and stood up. I let go of the handle and fell to the ground. I was frustrated, but found it sickly humorous that I had thought I could stand and walk. My parents had done so much for me. I wanted to do things on my own and not ask for assistance. Today was my brother Brian's birthday.

JOURNAL

2/14/2006: Lee and Uncle Roger went through his condo inventory together this morning. Roger brought over some Sneaky Pete's hot dogs. Therapy this morning was tough on Lee. He was very sore, probably due to his fall a few days ago. Aunt Patty came by to help Lee during this afternoon's therapy, and finished with him checking the mail. On their way out the door, they saw Beecher and Geraldine O., who gave Lee a crisp $100 bill.

DAVE

My boss, learning of the baseball memorabilia Lee had lost in the fire, asked me to deliver a gift from him to Lee. It was an autographed Ted Williams picture. I took it to Lee. His face lit up with excitement and gratefulness.

JOURNAL

2/16/2006: Lee has gained some weight and is now at 128 pounds. Tonight, Lee's buddy Dave brought him an awesome gift. Dave's boss, after hearing about Lee and the baseball memorabilia he lost in the fire, had decided to give Lee a Ted Williams autographed picture.

LEE

The picture is of the 1941 All-Star game when Ted Williams hit a walk off homerun to win the game. In the picture, Ted Williams, the Splendid Splinter is about to cross home plate and shake the hand of Joe DiMaggio. That December, Pearl Harbor was bombed and Ted Williams joined the Marine Corps. He served his country as a fighter pilot throughout World War II and again in Korea.

JOURNAL

2/17/2006: The home health nurse has not seen Lee in a week and can see a big difference in his wounds. We did the burn dressing today in less than 35 minutes.

HILARITY

JOURNAL

2/22/2006: Lee's therapist had him doing all kinds of stuff today, from walking to climbing steps to stretching to getting in and out of bed. Lee's work team came over and ate lunch with him today. They were all happy to see him.

LEE

Burn dressings became more painful as nerve endings grew more and more. The removal of bandages felt like my flesh was being ripped from my bones. I decided to make the best of it and tried to break the ice. As my mom was removing the bandage from by buttocks, I made a fart noise with my mouth at the precise moment she would have been directly in the line of fire. She looked up at me with a startled and almost angry look. Dad's face twisted into a grin, and I burst into laughter. "I made the noise with my mouth," I assured her, sending them both into loud peals of laughter.

"The human race has one really effective weapon, and that is laughter." **Mark Twain**

GRILLING

JOURNAL

3/11/2006: Lee and I decided to cook steaks for dinner. David is turkey hunting. Lee marinated the steaks and started the grill and got it ready for the meat. Lee put the steaks on the grill. I saw Lee put his hand into the flaming grill and panicked. Lee said that the steaks were burning and the tongs had fallen, so he flipped them with his hand because bending is still very difficult. When I asked him why he did that, Lee said he had to flip the steaks right then because they were burning.

LEE

I thought that since I already had scars over the majority of my body, one more would not hurt. If I could keep the steaks tender, I would sacrifice a new scar for it.

I saw pictures of my wounds earlier today and finally knew why my buttocks hurt so much.

JOURNAL

3/12/2006: Lee's Sunday school class came and had a class with him at our home today. Ashley V brought Lee a basket with goodies and a book, "Flags of Our Fathers," which Lee says is a book he had been wanting to read.

LEE

These books about World War II are stories of many people banding together for a common good. I greatly admire such tales of heroism and sacrifice. By reading about others facing tough times, I was able to gather strength through their stories.

JOURNAL

3/14/2006: Lee had a call today from Fireman T. Lawson who found and rescued Lee in his burning condo. They talked about that morning. Lee mentioned how eternally grateful he was for each and every fireman and for what they do.

LEE

There is something special to be said about those who go into harm's way to save others. There is no greater love than that. I will always be thankful and respectful of firemen and paramedics. Their profession is a noble one.

JOURNAL

3/16/2006: Lee saw Doctor Cross today. Lee has been having pain more than usual on the upper parts of his legs and asked Doctor Cross if he could do another skin graft. Doctor Cross said yes, so we are waiting to hear from the admissions office to see when we can get Lee in for another skin graft.

LEE

My upper thighs were causing me more pain than usual and seemed not to be healing as well as the wounds on my shins or stomach. I knew that after skin grafts, wounds seemed to heal faster, so I requested a ninth skin graft, and tenth surgery.

On March 16, 2006 an article about the fire was printed in the Birmingham News. Excerpts from the article:

Anne and David Lucas remember each moment of their son's Oct. 16 rescue from a burning Hoover condominium, from the encouraging words of a fire medic to the way their son's skin looked in a UAB Burn Center bed. "Like the inside of a barbeque grill lid," said David Lucas. "He smelled like smoke. His ears were full of soot," said Anne Lucas.

"Unlike other injuries, burns affect every organ," said UAB Burn Center Director Dr. Cross. "The body's metabolism typically doubles, sometimes for up to a year, as the body gears up to heal the wounds and fight infection," he said. "After a patient survives lung injury and any brain damage, his next hurdle is fighting malnutrition," he said.

Doctors who Lee met through overseas mission trips are among the vast network of supporters who keep tabs on his recovery. "Their presence the morning of the fire has helped the family cope," said Anne Lucas. "At times, there were more doctors visiting him than treating him," she said. "Every day, one of them was there, just checking his vital signs, asking what medicines and treatment were, and relaying that back to us."

"Burns like Lee's are among medicine's most impressive injuries, and ones seen less frequently with improvements in firefighting and building codes that contain the spread of fires," said Dr. Cross.

LEE

I had gotten to know several doctors and nurses from my church on overseas mission trips. They had given my family a more personal and down-to-earth explanation of what was happening as a result of my injuries, including what to expect next. There was a pediatrician, a retired pediatrician, a gynecologist, a cardiologist, an internist, a rheumatologist, and an anesthesiologist, along with many active and retired registered nurses.

I was a bit disheartened that the donor skin for my final graft was taken from my love handles. I had been having severe pain when I would sit or lie down, due to the burns on my buttocks. I was weak from the trauma I had endured and from my body healing, so I constantly wanted to sit down.

With skin graft wounds harvested from my love handles, sleeping would prove to be even more difficult. There was constant pain and discomfort.

JOURNAL

3/20/2006: Lee was admitted for another skin graft which is to take place tomorrow. Our friend, Joe C., asked Lee what he wanted for dinner. Lee answered immediately, "KFC, original recipe." Joe, along with his children, Jessica and Joey, brought us a bucket of chicken.

Lee's attitude about the surgery is, "Let's get it done."

3/21/2006: Lee got to see several of the nurses and burn dressing team today. They seemed pleased to know how he was doing. All the skin grafts were taking well.

3/21/2006: Doctor Cross stopped by and was pleased with the grafting. He remarked, *"Lee's body just really grabs that donor skin."*

3/24/2006: Lee was discharged. Total time in the hospital has now been 111 days.

3/27/2006: At a press conference today about our annual mission efforts to the Black

Belt, an extremely poor region in Alabama, Congressman Artur Davis mentioned Lee and his amazing testimony.

LEE

Members of my church would go and host a simple medical clinic at a church in the Black Belt region of Alabama. They would go to share hope through medicine and the caring for our fellow man. It did not matter if those who visited the clinic were Christian or not. It did not matter if those who came wanted to hear more about God. What mattered, what was important, was that our God was represented through the love and willingness of believers to serve others.

JOURNAL

3/29/2006: I told Lee how proud we are of him for the way he is handling the accident and the pain. Lee replied, "What else can I do?!" Intrigued, I thought that Lee could be a very difficult patient if he wanted. But instead, he had made the choice to be serene and understanding.

MY CHURCH

JOURNAL

4/9/2006: Today was Lee's first Sunday back at church. As he made his way up the walkway into the front door, he was greeted by a smiling Geraldine O. and Mary J. Many people hugged and/or patted Lee on the back for going through such a trying time with an utter willingness to make a full recovery. Brother Scott mentioned that Lee was in the crowd. Lee received a standing ovation for his perseverance, strength and determination. Mostly, though, the applause was meant to praise God for what He had done in all of our lives, and for Lee.

LEE

I did not want to spend my life recovering from something when I could make a concentrated effort to get better. I almost understood why people kept telling me I was brave, but it didn't seem to make sense. The truth is, I knew I could not give up.

JOURNAL

5/3/2006: Lee told David this afternoon that he planned to visit the bowling alley tonight. Lee's bowling buddies have visited him every Wednesday before bowling since he was in Spain rehab. Everyone was very happy to see Lee.

LEE

At the bowling alley, people were coming up and shaking my hand as I sat in my wheel-chair. I was electrified with pleasure, happy to once again be in a place where true competition resides.

JOURNAL

5/8/2006: Today, the 13th Annual Alabama Fire Sprinkler Associations' Tony Bice Memorial Burn Center Golf Tournament Invitational and dinner was held at Pine Tree Country Club. Donations to this fund are used by the Burn Survivor team to help with patients, like Lee. It helps with burn education and other burn patient support. Lee was the guest speaker.

LEE

I was rolled in my wheel-chair to the podium. I spoke of how important it was to educate others about burn education and about how important the Burn Survivor Team was to my ongoing recovery. I spoke of the integral part the team would play in future burn survivor recoveries.

RETURNING TO WORK

JOURNAL

5/11/2006: This morning Lee returned to work part time. Lee's team met him outside as we pulled up. They held signs welcoming him back and everyone in his department brought food to celebrate. Lee was also given a money wreath. When we asked him how much it was, he smiled gratefully and would not say. Lee's team had also started a "White Sox Tuesday." Every Tuesday since the fire, they had worn white socks to work. Each member who wore white socks on that day of the week placed two dollars into a fund to give to Lee when he returned to work. When I spoke to a nurse friend of mine in the UAB trauma unit about his return to work, she said that with the extent of his injuries, he should still be in the hospital.

When Lee got home, I had so many questions about his day. However, he just replied "Everything went fine." Tonight, his bowling buddies Dave and George visited. Their league had ended, and they brought Lee his share of the prize fund.

JOURNAL

5/19/2006: Aunt Patty and I did Lee's burn dressing today. During the dressing change, we talked about how well the wounds were healing. Lee said, "Why not talk about it after the dressing change is done?!"

LEE

I was standing naked with open wounds over my body while two women were chatting about something that did not move the dressing change forward. I was ready for the dressing change to be done.

JOURNAL

5/20/2006: Today we stopped by Hoover Fire station #4, the primary station that responded to Lee's fire. Lee got to meet one of the firemen who helped carry him out of the building. All of the firemen and paramedics were very excited to see Lee and told him he could come back to visit whenever he wanted. The firemen gave Lee a Hoover Fire Station golf shirt, which Lee said he was proud to accept.

6/1/2006: At therapy today, Lee walked 1,540

feet with his walker and bent one of his knees 90 degrees. He was almost able to bend his other knee 90 degrees, but he could not get all the way there.

6/8/2006: Lee's occupation and physical therapist at Spain rehab discharged him. He will be doing therapy only at home from now on.

LEE S.

I remember Lee being so excited the day he could tie his own shoes. Successes as simple as that become a special achievement and really make us appreciate the intense recovery he went through.

"Success consists of going from failure to failure without the loss of enthusiasm."
Winston Churchill

JOURNAL

6/14/2006: Lee's co-workers told me that Lee is up walking around the office more and more. They keep a close eye on him.

6/15/2006: Lee's burn dressing appointment at UAB today went well. Afterwards, Lee suggested we go to the 9th floor trauma burn unit. As we wheeled through the waiting room into the trauma bay, Lee said, "Stop!" He stood up from his wheelchair and walked into the burn dressing change room. Lee was surrounded by the burn dressing team who were elated at how well he is doing. Melvin was excited to see him walking. He asked Lee if he could talk to a burn patient for him.

Lee said, "Sure."

6/22/2006: Lee got out of his bed by himself today. This morning, he asked for five to ten more minutes of sleep. When I went down after those extra minutes, Lee was standing there in his room on his own.

A FINE HOUR

JASON, CHILDHOOD FRIEND

I was getting married and asked Lee to be my best man. Lee still had open wounds that were extremely painful, and was easily fatigued, but he accepted. July 1, 2006 was my wedding day. Lee and I walked out together. Lee wobbled and hobbled while holding onto his cane and stood with all his pain by my side as I got married. This was a testament to Lee's character, and it meant a lot to me, personally. I had not seen Lee stand for so long since the accident.

JOURNAL

7/1/2006: Lee was honored today to be best man in his friend Jason's wedding.

LEE

I was a bit concerned. As best man in Jason's wedding, I would have to stand for 30 minutes unassisted while leaning on a cane, and escort the maid of honor. I decided to give all 118% of my effort. I stood with sweat running down my face and shaking for 30 plus minutes unassisted, leaning on my cane, escorted the maid of honor out, and then happily fell into my wheel chair. This was the first time since the fire that I stood unassisted for 30 minutes. It was also my first time to ever be the best man in a wedding.

JOURNAL

7/4/2006: Today, as we were heading to eat family lunch, Lee asked for his car keys and said he was driving. He climbed into his vehicle, negotiated the clutch and five speed well, and drove to his Uncle Darell's and Aunt Dale's for lunch. Afterwards, he drove back and began packing. He does not have any immediate plans to move, but he wanted to get things ready for when that day comes.

JOURNAL

7/6/2006: This morning Lee told David he was going to get out of the vehicle at work by himself, gather his backpack and cane into his wheelchair, then wheel himself into the building.

JOURNAL

7/13/2006: Lee drove his dad's truck to work today as I rode in the passenger seat. He did just fine.

7/16/2006: Lee did what he called "driving therapy" and drove to work by himself to prepare for driving alone Monday.

7/17/2006: Lee drove himself to and from work today.

JOURNAL

7/26/2006: A lady in Lee's office walked by his desk today and was surprised to see him sitting in his office chair rather than in his wheelchair. This kind lady told Lee what an inspiration he is to her.

JOURNAL

7/28/2006: Today Lee received a call from the Mayor of Hoover, Alabama, thanking him for a letter he had written praising the firemen who saved him.

LEE

Sometime earlier, I had written a letter to the Mayor of the City of Hoover, Alabama. I asked him directly for the firemen and paramedics who responded to the fire in the early morning hours of October 16, 2005 to be publicly recognized for their brave and selfless efforts that saved my life.

JOURNAL

8/10/2006: Lee removed most of his bandages for his dressing change today. We think we are about to be fired. Lee really wants to do the dressing changes on his own.

8/17/2006: Lee has stopped using his wheelchair today and is going to and from places using his cane or walker.

8/31/2006: Tonight is opening night of Lee's league at the bowling alley. Lee said everyone was excited to see him walk in there on his own to support them.

9/4/2006: Lee was grilling tonight. He bent over and picked the tongs up rather than sticking his hand into the fire to flip the steaks.

COOKING

Hebrews 10:32 (NIV), *"Remember those earlier days after you had received the light, when you endured in a great conflict full of suffering."*

LEE

On the one year anniversary of the fire, October 16, 2006, I was by myself and decided to cook some red meat on the grill to celebrate the day when I was cooked well enough to eat.

The idea was meant at first to be a joke, but afterwards, I was glad I decided to celebrate the time I was burned, instead of attempting to deny it. Grilling has become a wryly funny type of therapy, and has even become a learning experience for me. Grilling red meat has become an annual event. Every year on October 16, I will be burning some sort of red meat over an open flame and eating it. I do it to commemorate and to celebrate with good humor the day that has been forever charred into my life.

"To truly laugh, you must be able to take your pain, and play with it!" **Charlie Chaplin**

JOURNAL

12/24/2006: Today Lee had lunch with his buddy Carter H. who is about to be sent for his second tour to Iraq.

12/27/2006: Lee was able to bowl tonight. This time last year, Lee was having trouble walking due to a pressure sore on his foot.

Bowling was extremely difficult. Add to this the fact that I was not able to put up the type of score I once could. I was not too happy. But I was able to roll a ball down a sixty foot lane, which was a major success.

LEE S.

As far as I'm concerned, the greatest day was the day Lee started bowling again. You could tell it was difficult for him, but the fact that he was *doing it,* is what was great!

JOURNAL

2/12/2007: Lee gracefully told David and me that our services are no longer needed to do burn dressings. He will be doing them on his own.

Jeremiah 10:19 (NIV), *"Woe to me because of my injury! My wounds are incurable! Yet I said to myself, this is my sickness, and I must endure it."*

LEE

As soon as I was physically flexible enough, I decided to do burn dressing changes myself. I had become the dressing change nurse and the patient. These actions were very liberating, and as far as I am concerned, offered a unique perspective on what was happening, along with providing a new type of therapy.

I was happy to not need assistance while taking care of my wounds. I was glad I was able to stomach the pain caused by my own hand better. I was happy these dressing changes would now be done exclusively by me.

During the next nine months, I self-performed burn dressings every other day. I did them just as they had been done in the past. I started by clipping off the bandages. Second, I washed my wounds with soap in the shower. Third, I would bandage myself. The pain was easier to tolerate because I was causing it. The mandated stretching needed to accomplish the task of a dressing change also greatly helped me in my regular therapy sessions. It was not only the movement required to complete the dressing change, but also the focus and accuracy needed to place the bandages properly over my open wounds. I cooked out as much as I possibly could.

VIII. Home continued

JOURNAL

11/24/2007: Today Claudia, Julia and, I visited Hoover Fire Station #4. Claudia and Julia told the firemen "Thank you for rescuing Uncle Lee-Lee!"

LEE

Burn dressings were getting quicker now. I had gotten the time down to twelve minutes. The wounds on both legs, from my thigh to my foot, had closed. The wounds on my arms had completely healed. The majority of my stomach and buttocks wounds had healed, but each had a large open wound remaining.

I was helping pull down the Christmas

decorations from the attic. I had the box the tree was in. I was guiding the box with the tree down the steps by pulling it. The box slid into my shins, and what resulted was an eerie and somewhat familiar pulsating and maddening pain. It was extremely excruciating, lightning-quick throbbing sting as if someone were brutally beating my shins like drums.

JOURNAL

12/8/2007: Last night Lee, David, and I had dinner with the Lawson family. T. Lawson was the first fireman to reach Lee in his burning condo. We met his wife, children, and mother.

LEE

In early 2008, I was in line at Wal-Mart. A mother and young child stood in front of me. This child was probably five or six years old. He was picking up candy, batteries, magazines, and anything else he could find, and asking if he could have them. The frustrated mother replied "no" repetitively.

Bored, the young child looked at my forearm. He saw my skin graft scar, pointed and asked "What is that?"

I looked at the child eagerly and replied, "This is what happens when you do not listen to your mother."

The child looked startled. He looked at his mom, and then back at me, and then moved away and began politely conversing with the cashier. The mom looked at me with an embarrassed, but thankful grin on her face.

AN ESCAPE FROM WHAT I HAVE RECENTLY KNOWN

JOURNAL

4/28/2008: Lee is having dinner with the Burgess family in Washington D.C. tonight. Lee is on his first vacation since the fire. When I asked, he said that we could not go with him.

JOURNAL

5/5/2008: Lee is home from his trip to D.C. We are thankful for friends David O., the Burgess family, Michael B, and Congressman Artur Davis who met with Lee as he visited our nation's capital.

LEE

The only open wound I could see or feel with my hands was about the size of a quarter. It was on the top of the back of my left leg where my leg and buttocks met.

JOURNAL

5/29/2008: Today, Doctor Cross, Lee's burn doctor, discharged him. All of Lee's wounds have closed. He still has a lot of stretching limitations, but is coming along well. Time under Doctor Cross's care was two years, seven months and 13 days.

LEE

In June 2008, I had the great privilege of recording a video about what God has done for me and my family through a ministry called "I AM SECOND." If you would like to watch any of these videos visit iamsecond.com.

One Sunday, late in the summer of 2008, I was asked by our church's children's minister, Lyn H., to come and speak with the elementary school kids. I went and told them as lightly as I could about being burned, and the pain, and what it took to make it through, and then asked for questions.

Several hands shot up. The number one question was, "Do you have any cool scars?" I showed them my shins.

The room was filled with cries of, "Yuck!" and "Cool!"

BROTHER NATE

Now, after seeing Lee walking and carrying on as if nothing had ever happened, I begin to wonder about what other miracles God will work for those who place their faith in Him?

A GREAT HONOR

JOURNAL

9/21/2008: Today Lee and several others were honored to have their pictures hung in the lobby of Spain Rehab Center in downtown Birmingham, Alabama. This ceremony was referred to as a photographic tribute to "The Prevailing Spirit of Patients at SRC" to offer photographic encouragement to others. It was given courtesy of Rick Garlikov studios in Birmingham, Alabama. Lee's photo is on the pillar directly in front of the elevator in the main lobby of Spain Rehab.

LEE

The picture is of me playing chess on a board with pieces that survived the fire. I wanted a picture playing chess because of the fact that the chess board given to me by my friends was donated to the stack of games for recreational therapy at Spain Rehab. Playing chess was my final way of proving that I did not have the anoxic brain injury that all of my doctors predicted I would have. This picture of me playing chess stands as a reminder that God does perform miracles.

Psalm 35:18 (NIV), *"I will give you thanks in the great assembly; among the throngs I will praise you."*

LEE

On July 29, 2009, The City of Hoover held a ceremony. I had the great honor and privilege to pin a Medal of Valor to each fireman, paramedic, and police officer who responded to the fire. This was the one moment I had greatly anticipated. I had wanted each individual who responded to the fire to be publicly recognized for their actions. And, of course, all who received a medal said they would trade it for another chance to save one more life. What a special crop of people. They are a living testament to courage.

The following is an excerpt from a speech I gave at the ceremony:

"Because all of these guys risked their lives for the chance to save another, I am standing here today. There is no greater love that one can show than risking his or her life for another. I am extremely thankful that you guys are being publicly recognized. This day is about honoring you."

Today was also the day of the birth for my good friend Owens's first child. The baby was premature, weighing only one pound eleven ounces.

After the recognition ceremony, I picked up some barbeque ribs from Dreamland BBQ in downtown Birmingham and took them to the hospital for Owen, his wife Jessica and me to eat lunch after the birth of their first child. Today, after being born at one pound eleven ounces, on a day I will never forget, the child is running strong.

Today was my buddy John's birthday

FOLKS

OWEN

Lee was himself again! His wounds have healed and he has a great outlook on life. Lee is sharing his story as a testimony, and he is rededicating his life to the Lord by explaining what has been done for him. Whenever I think about him, I thank God for saving my friend.

JASON

Every moment we can make the choice to become a better person and to appreciate everything around us. Lee's experience has shown me how wonderful our family and friends are, and that they are not to be taken for granted, because you never know when they will be taken away. God has a plan, but sometimes we have to go through things, or see family or friends go through them, to appreciate His grace and mercy.

GEORGE

Lee was able to overcome adversity due to his attitude and his confidence. He had an amazing support team of family members and friends.

DAVE

Lee's accident was horrible, but it brought out and illustrated the best in everyone. Lee's parents were examples to everyone due to their unshakable faith.

DOCTOR BANKS

From the first day forward, God's hand worked. The doctors were surprised when the CT scan did not show brain damage. The study of medicine said it should have. Then Lee's lungs began to function normally. The weeks passed with suffering, with debridement, and with slow pulmonary improvement. Survival was accomplished by a miracle from God, and the support of modern medicine. God's hand clearly moved for Lee's healing, and for those who prayed, He demonstrated His power in a way that is life changing. A miracle, and the power of answered prayer, should never be forgotten or underestimated.

DOCTOR WATTERSON

One thing I learned through Lee's recovery is in the context of prayer for another human being. Whether the prayer be for their welfare in any way, or for their soul particularly that, if tears are shed and the faithful pouring out of one's soul in prayer occurs, take heed, because something is about to happen.

DOCTOR FOSTER

The night Lee Lucas was burned seemed like a real tragedy. I know now that the greatest tragedy would be two-fold: if Lee's story was not told and, if the awesomeness of the God we serve was not recognized. Any attempt for anyone to try to take credit for what happened would take away from the power of the Living God. Only He could have orchestrated such an amazing event. God was the strength and the courage of the firefighters. God was the wisdom and the skilled hands of the nurses, doctors and therapists who worked with Lee. It was His great power that strengthened Lee's caring family. His power empowered those who faithfully prayed for Lee and loved him and his family.

G. BURNS, BURN CHARGE NURSE

The burn dressing changes are nothing but a memory now, and this event in Lee's life is just history. Lee made the best of it all and now is making even better of it. He has chosen to tell the story that most want to forget.

IX. Insights on Recovery

"Have the patience to hear me out and I will tell you what I'm all about."

Joseph Plumb Martin, **Private Yankee Doodle** ii

1 John 5: 9-10 (NIV), "*9: We accept man's testimony, but God's testimony is greater because it is the testimony of God, which he has given about his Son. Anyone who believes in the Son of God has this testimony is his heart.*"

I do not know what the future holds.

This is what I recall thinking shortly after I had awakened in the hospital. Of course, no one knows what the future holds, and no one knows when their time will come. But you can somewhat gauge tomorrow based upon what is going on today. Lying in my hospital bed with pain in every single movement, with extreme grogginess from all of the meds I was on, having to have someone assist me with everything, and not having any sense of reason as to why I had been burned, my future seemed terrifying. There was a great fear of what was coming next. I could not move without uncompromising pain, and would remain that way for the foreseeable future. I was horrified.

All through the wicked pain and decimating agony of burns over the majority of my body, all I knew was that I could not give up. I had a new chance at life, but I needed something to bring it all together. This mind frame eventually led me to start to make some sort of plan to get home. I saw a great divide and was able to envision the way to recovery-an ending. All that was needed was to find a way to bridge the gap between that divide to make a full recovery.

Psalm 119:105(NIV), *"Your word is a lamp to my feet and a light for my path."*

The task of bridging the gap to a recovery looked dark and bleak. Something was needed to help, because it would be impossible to make a full recovery alone. After much doubt and fear about what was coming next, I made a decision to dedicate this struggle to God and ask Him to help me.

DESIRE

1 Peter 4:12(NIV)

"Dear friends, do not be surprised at the painful trial you are suffering, as though something strange were happening to you."

In the hospital, I remember thinking that I did not ever want to be in a place again that resembled where I was. I forged a deep revulsion and disgust. What I desired, with all my being, was to be completely recovered and nothing less. Regardless of what or how long it took, I would be completely recovered or spend the rest of my life trying. A commitment was made by me to accept what had happened instead of running from it. This decision led me to take on the task of continuously working today, while looking forward to tomorrow with full recovery and complete independence as the end goal.

At this time, I formed what may seem like an overly confident attitude. It was an attitude that said with Jesus in my heart, I can take anything that is thrown at me, for I proclaim to God that this will not be my ending. This will be the time when I will meet and learn to defeat any struggle with a fighting faith that will endure through it all. Regardless of the outcome, I have the faith needed to persevere through anything. In the end, whether I am alive and standing or not, I will have finished my race because I have kept my faith in Jesus Christ. This defines a fighting faith.

COMMITMENT

Matthew 6:34(NIV)

"Therefore do not worry about tomorrow, for tomorrow will worry about itself. Each day has enough trouble on its own."

Asking why something happened is normal and expected. In a way, it is something that must occur. Asking why exhibits a principle of acceptance, and is attributable to the mourning process, but can be harmful to your overall rehabilitation if allowed to fester out of control. Asking why refers to something that is in the past. Ultimately, when experiencing a trying time, asking why drains valuable brain power that is sorely needed for healing, and it can cloud your overall renewal of your life. Asking why is a justified question. But there is one undisputable fact-the fact that regardless of the reasons why, you are going through your trying time anyway. So why not save asking why for some time later?

During this anxious and troubling era, it will

feel as though you are lost in your own wilderness of pain and fear, locked inside a wasteland where you must decide how to get out. You have to determine what you will use to find a way and look for any means to assist you in your journey. You must rely on all the resources you have access to and make the best of them. You must not give up.

One resource that we all have access to is a belief or a faith, a conviction that says "I need help," an intercession, a guide to help us get through this maze riddled with pain and doubt and fear. You must rely upon what you know and what you have irrevocable access to-to something that is yours and yours alone unless you decide to give it up.

If your belief says that you do need help and redemption, then you are experiencing a clearer view of your reality. You will then be faced with the decision as to what your next step will be based upon what is happening, and you must seek out that which will get you through.

When I had that realization, that clarifying view, a light bulb went off in my head. The way to make it through became blatantly obvious. This clear and obvious way to victory is a faith that cannot be shaken, a belief that can withstand anything, one that will grow in the harshest of conditions. This is a faith that will transform your inhospitable surroundings into your own personal place of peace.

Visualize complete rehabilitation and make a commitment to work through it all. Use what you envisioned to ignite what you need to do to make a full recovery.

Envision what you desire, remember that desire, and do not forget that "your end vision drives you to attempt great things in faith you would not otherwise do." **Steve Smith, <u>T4T, A Discipleship Re-Revolution</u>**iii

All I ask is that you keep your faith while going through your personal struggle. For by faith many are drawn to the word of God. For by faith many who would not otherwise do so will believe because you have kept your faith. For by faith the world will change.

When you hold true to your faith you will be an example of pure freedom.

"I do not know what the future holds, but I know who holds the future."
Doctor Martin Luther King Jr.

FAITH

Hebrews 11:1(NIV)

"Now faith is confidence in what we hope for and assurance about what we do not see."

What works is faith-a belief that is rock solid and cannot be broken or cracked if you fall or have a setback. A faith that acts as a refinery, a simple faith that finds a way to take all negative thoughts and emotions and forges or recycles them into something that can be useful for your recovery. Have a faith that will strengthen through your own suffering. Have a fighting faith.

What this faith is in is up to you and you alone. You must decide for yourself what to believe in. But, what did it for me is a fighting faith. What I relied upon was a faith in Jesus Christ.

Proverbs 3:3 (NIV), *"Let love and faithfulness never leave you; bind them around your neck, write them on the tablet of your heart."*

Making any type of commitment is much easier than keeping it, for it is much easier to start the race than to finish it. I suggest having some sort of reminder or trigger that keeps your burning desire to stay the course alive. Write something down to remind you, use a picture or something you see every day to represent and encourage the keeping of your faith, and remember that encouragement. For me, I had a poster on the wall of my condominium bedroom that I saw every day. It was burned. The poster was of the Iwo Jima Memorial in Washington D.C., with a caption at the bottom that read, "Fortitude: the strength to persist, the courage to endure."

BELIEF

Jeremiah 6:16(NIV)
"Stand at the crossroads and look; ask for the ancient paths, ask where the good way is, and walk in it and you will find rest for your soul."

Give thanks to everyone who plays a part in your trying time. It may seem as though a cruel joke is being played on you. It may feel as though everything is working against you or that nothing you do is helping. This is not the time to jump to conclusions. This is the time to be patient and wait while not letting go of your beliefs.

Focus on your core principles, on your personal values, those things that form the foundation of who you are. When the world seems to be against you, and you feel as if your soul is being tried, hold fast and never let go of your faithful beliefs. Adhere to the common denominator that defines you, and rebuild upon it.

This is much harder than it sounds. At a time in which you are faced with the emotion of your present surroundings, it is very easy to act upon your feelings instead of focusing on that which will get you through. And if you act upon that emotion and do something that causes a setback, do not get discouraged. Get up! Focus on the solution. Press on and seek the Holy Spirit because your journey is not yet over.

Quiet your mind, focus and become subconsciously still, yearn with your soul to feel the whispering wind of the Holy Spirit and you will find your place of peace. Within this peace a mighty warrior will emerge. This is a bold warrior who fights with Jesus Christ at his center. This is a warrior who has a fighting faith.

TRUTH

Isaiah 53: 4- 5 (NIV)

"Surely he took up our pain and bore our suffering, yet we considered him punished by God, stricken by him, and afflicted. But he was pierced for our transgressions, he was crushed for our iniquities; the punishment that brought us peace was on him, and by his wounds we are healed."

Him whose punishment brought us peace is Jesus Christ.

A true belief in Jesus Christ will make miracles happen.

How can you explain the fact that with a carbon monoxide level of 37.4% I lived without any brain damage? How can you explain the fact that in my burning condo, I collapsed at the precise place that was the safest and most survivable in that raging inferno? How can you explain the fact that I had the very best network of family and friends, many who faithfully prayed, brought food, stayed with me and comforted my family and me and reminded us all that we were not alone?

I believe that afore mentioned, and many other things that occurred that night and the weeks and months and years to follow, are no coincidence. I believe that these are signs that there is a greater power to be acknowledged, and I believe that there is a greater God than we here on Earth can possibly fathom. This God I am speaking of is the God of faith. This God of faith is Jesus Christ.

You may ask how someone believes in this God of faith. How does someone believe in Jesus Christ? You might ask how someone believes in this God of love and compassion that can drive one to attempt great things.

This God of great power and awe! You ask how a person can believe in this God who can lead someone who is lost in their own wilderness, in this God who can guide someone through their wasteland of fear and doubt.

Genesis 1: 27 (NIV)
"God created mankind in his own image, in the

image of God he created them; male and female he created them."

In the beginning, God and man lived together in harmony. God and man lived in a place of heavenly characteristics, a place in which all things were right and true.

Man then rebelled against God. Man succeeded in creating a great divide between himself and God.

God desired to be one with man again. Man discovered that he was alone without God.

Man came to realize the distinct nature of what was happening. Man determined that he was lost, and he was seeking a way to be one with God again.

John 14: 6 (NIV)

Jesus said: "I am the way the truth and the life. No one comes to the Father except through me."

God sent his only son Jesus Christ to die for us all to pay for man's disobedience against Him. God then raised Jesus from the dead three days later to conquer death and to show His Truth as it was written.

1 Corinthians 15: 3-5 (NIV)

"For what I received I passed on to you as of first importance: that Christ died for our sins according to the scriptures, that he was buried, that he was raised on the third day according to the scripture."

At this moment, man began to understand and gather his bearings.

Man starts to realize where he is, and the many directions he can move. Next he decides, specifically, which path to follow, and then generates a determination to navigate through his own personal wilderness of pain.

Romans 10: 9 (NIV)

"If you confess with your mouth, "Jesus is Lord," and believe in your heart that God raised him from the dead, you will be saved."

Man then realized that the need for truth, for

healing and redemption was contingent upon a decision to follow Christ, and that he needed Him to help bear the burden. Man realized that to become one with God again is to become one with Jesus Christ.

1 Timothy 2: 3-6 (NIV)

"This is good, and pleases God our savior, who wants all men to be saved and to come to the knowledge of the truth. For there is one God and one mediator between God and man, the man Christ Jesus, who gave himself as a ransom for all people."

Remember this simple formula: First, a realization of a problem or issue and that some sort of solid transforming help is needed. Second, it is necessary to have a deep desire to change or recuperate and do whatever is necessary to become rehabilitated. Third, we need an eager strength of mind to see it all through regardless of what happens, or how long it all takes.

The acceptance of Jesus Christ in your life represents the bridge needed to become one with

God again. A belief in Jesus Christ will give you a direct link to God.

When man follows his commitment to stay true to Jesus Christ, he will accomplish great things. When one decides that a unique determination to be with One who knows no secession, the world will change.

Although many do not want to or are afraid to make this decision, it is simple and easy, and is for everyone. Put God, Jesus Christ first in everything you do. Love and respect God first; next treat people like you would want to be treated. When you do these you will unearth a keen determination to directly and indirectly spread the word of God.

With this simple understanding, believing that you can do anything through Christ who gives you strength becomes second nature.

YOU

Psalm 77:11(NIV)

"I will remember the deeds of the Lord; yes, I will remember your miracles from long ago."

Give thanks in all circumstances, decide whether or not to make a commitment to something greater than yourself, and keep that faithful commitment regardless of how long it takes or who approves or disapproves of it.

If you make the decision to commit to do this, and if you honor that commitment regardless of the outcome, in the end you will completely conquer the struggle that is occurring within because you have kept your binding faith.

If you make the decision to accept Jesus Christ into your heart, say something similar to the following prayer: "God, thank you for loving me even though I have rebelled against you. I believe that your son Jesus died on a cross for me and that you raised him from the dead. I now put my faith in Jesus, I ask for Jesus to save me, to forgive me for my trespassing mutinies against you. I confess that Jesus is Lord. Amen."

Make sure any decision made about what you believe is yours and yours alone. This makes the decision unique and historic to you, and it also allows a remembrance you can summon to tell others about your momentous decision and the personal and meaningful circumstances that surrounded it. Additionally, this time in your life acts as a new foundation to build upon, a new basis in which you can use the things that represented your life beforehand to help encourage others in their time of need. This time represents a settling of a groundwork expressing the exact moment the conclusion you determined was needed manifested itself.

Your time will be difficult and confusing with a lack of focus. This is why the decision about which path to follow must be your own.

If this story of being burned and the recovery that followed helps someone decide to accept Jesus Christ into their heart, then going through it was worth it. If this story of being burned and of the following recovery leads someone to rededicate their life to Christ, then it was worth it. Will you be that someone?

Mark 1:17 (NIV), *"Come, follow me,"* said *Jesus, "and I will send you out to fish for people."*

THE FUTURE

Deuteronomy 4:9(NIV)

"Be careful, and watch yourself closely so that you do not forget the things your eyes have seen or let them slip from your heart as long as you live."

Prayer

Lord, thank You for all that you have done. Thank You for those brave firemen and paramedics who saved my life. Thank You for the wisdom of each and every doctor and nurse who worked on and with me. Thank You for my family and friends, to all who took time out of their lives to comfort my family and me. Thank You, God, for saving my life. Regardless of the individual traits of each person, please move in their hearts to make a decision about You in their lives. Please use this story of Your glory to assist in accomplishing this. Please give us all the strength and the fortitude to press on in whatever endeavor we may each be facing. Please instill into each and every person that they have a choice to make a decision to follow You. Thank You for giving me the clarity to make my own decision to follow You. And thank You, God, for giving us all the privilege and independent right of deciding for ourselves what to believe. To You all glory is given. Amen!

1 Corinthians 12:25-26(NIV)

"So that there should be no division in the body, but that its parts have equal concern for each other. If one part suffers, every part suffers with it; if one part is honored, every part rejoices with it."

I believe that at this very moment there is a renaissance type of movement occurring. It is a mass revival, a restoration of God; a recovery of a loving relationship with Jesus is catching fire and spreading all over the world. We are living in a time when I see an understanding of God that passes through all Christian denominations and, all political leanings, a time when people are focusing on their common love for Jesus Christ.

Matthew 5: 17 (NIV)

Jesus Said, "Do not think that I have come to abolish the Law or the Prophets; I have not come to abolish them but to fulfill them."

I see on the horizon, people coming back to the true fundamental foundations of Christianity by following Jesus and the truth that is in His Word. I see a people coming together in one cause: the cause of Jesus Christ.

Psalm 119:45 (NIV), *"I will walk about in freedom, for I have sought out your precepts."*

Your decision is autonomous because it comes from within. The choice is yours. You make the decision, you are the one who is responsible for your faith, and you are the one who either decides to accept or deny the free gift of salvation that comes through Jesus Christ. You are the one who determines what is needed to overcome your struggle that is occurring within.

Our futures are not yet set, our time is not yet over, and our faith is what will hold the test of our time. Your realization of reality will help you accept what is going on in your life. Your determination to hold fast by clinging to an acceptance based upon this moment of clarity will speak volumes about you to yourself and to others. Your honoring of your commitment will test the times and stand as a beacon for others who will one day face a similar struggle, who will one day be lost in a wilderness, and who will one day be seeking a way out.

2 Corinthians 1:34(NIV)

"Praise be to the God and Father of our Lord Jesus Christ, the Father of compassion and the God of all comfort, who comforts us in all our troubles, so that we can comfort those in any trouble with the comfort we ourselves have received from God."

We each have a unique story about the life we are living. We each have a unique story of the adverse tests that we have each made it through. What is learned by your personal story and what can be drawn from it is what makes an impact upon others who will hear it.

Tell your story of the acceptance of Jesus

into your heart. Remember how things were before you decided to accept Jesus. Tell of the circumstances surrounding the moment in which you realized the truth by not forgetting the very instance in which you made the choice to get through your terrifyingly anxious and demanding time. Use this context to let others know of your decision. Tell the story of when you said yes to Jesus Christ.

When you make a decision to follow Jesus Christ you will realize that his love and the following of his commandments are meant for you. All you have to do is accept Him into your heart. Will you open your heart to Him? Will you accept Jesus?

In final summation: "I do not know what the future holds, but I know who holds the future" It is YOU!

If you would like to hear about how to attain a faith in Jesus Christ or hear stories of how others have experienced God in their lives, visit iamsecond.com.

If you would like to watch my interview about the fire check out: www.iamsecond.com/seconds/lee-lucas/

If you would like to learn how to disciple others please visit t4tonline.org

If you would like to hear a radio interview I gave about the fire check out: http://openhousecommunity.com.au/player/?listenid=11381

PHOTOGRAPHS

Picture of the outside of my condominium unit on the second floor.

Picture is of the hallway from my front door looking down the hallway into my spare bedroom.

Picture of the stove top next door where the fire started

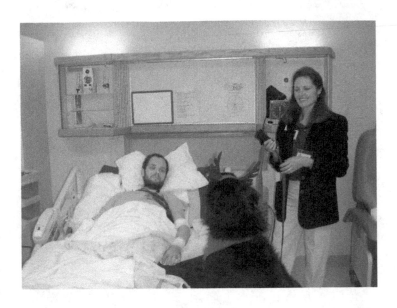

Bailey the therapy dog visiting Lee on Christmas Eve with Aunt Patty

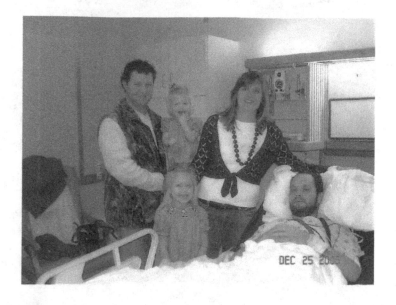

Brian, April, Claudia and Julia with Lee on Christmas Day.

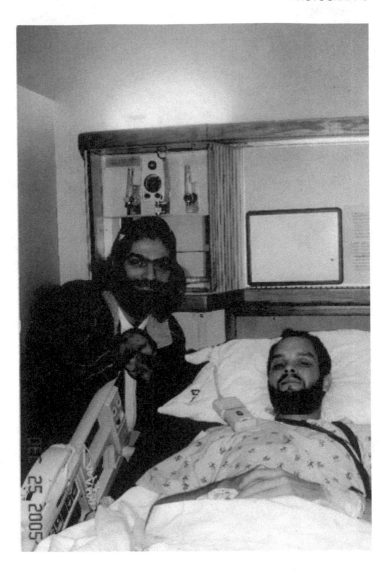

George and Lee on Christmas Day

Melvin and Lee

Lee's return to work

The moment Lee was presented the money wreath upon his return to work. Dad is in the back ground.

T. Lawson and R. Morton, the firemen who rescued Lee from his burning condo. Lawson is up front and Morton is in the back.

Congressman Artur Davis and Lee

Doctor Cross and Lee at the Tony Bice Memorial Golf Tournament.

Nieces Claudia & Julia Visiting Hoover Fire Station #4 on 11/24/2007

This is the picture hanging in the main lobby of Spain Rehab in Birmingham Alabama, and it is the cover of this book; it was taken courtesy of Rick Garlikov Studios in Birmingham Alabama.

INDEX

300 Bowling score: A 300 score in bowling is a perfect game and the highest score possible in the game of bowling. This score represents a game in which the bowler gets 12 strikes in the same game.

A

Alabama Fire Sprinkler Association, alfiresprinkler.org, The Alabama Fire Sprinkler Association is comprised of fire sprinkler contractors, industry suppliers and code officials as well as representatives from other associated organizations and individuals involved with or affected by fire sprinkler issues

Alexandre Dumas, French Novelist, born in modern day Haiti in 1802, Author of many classics including "The Count of Monte Cristo" and "The Three Musketeers"

(ALCS) American League Championship Series: in the game of baseball, the matchup that determines which team of the American League goes to the World Series.

Amazing Grace: A Christian hymn published in 1779.

Anesthesiologist: a medical doctor trained in anesthesia and perioperative medicine.

Anoxic brain injury: An injury caused by the lack of oxygen to the brain. Brain cells without enough oxygen will begin to die after about four minutes.

B

Brian Tracy: A leading self-development author and coach in the United States, born in Canada in 1944.

Black Belt Region: In the U.S. state of Alabama, refers to the region's rich black topsoil. The Black Belt Region of Alabama is one of the poorest regions in America.

Bronchoscope: A thin, flexible instrument with a lighted viewing tube that is used to visualize the air passages to the lungs.

Burn unit: A ward or part thereof in which beds are used exclusively for treating patients with significant burns.

C

Carboxyhemoglobin: A compound formed in the blood by the binding of carbon monoxide to hemoglobin. It is stable and therefore cannot absorb or transport oxygen.

Cardiologist: A medical doctor who specializes in diagnosing and treating disease or conditions of the heart and blood vessels-the cardiovascular system.

Caring Bridge: CaringBridge.org, a website that is mostly used as a personal health journal, rallying friends and family during any type of health journey.

Charlie Chaplin: British comedian born in 1889. Iconic figure in the silent film age.

CT scan: Computed tomography scan. Detailed

images of internal organs are obtained by this type of sophisticated X-ray device. CT stands for computed tomography. A CT scan can reveal anatomic details of internal organs that cannot be seen in conventional X-rays.

D

Doctor Martin Luther King, Jr.: American Baptist Minister, Civil Rights Leader, Nobel Prize Winner, born 1929.

Dreamland BBQ: Founded in 1958 in a small shack in Tuscaloosa Alabama. Dreamland has several locations across the Southeast.

E

Edgar Allan Poe: American writer, poet, critic and editor, Born 1809

F

Flags of our Fathers: Book, 2000, Movie, 2006. American story of the soldiers who raised the flag at battle of Iwo Jima in 1945.

Frederick Douglas: Former American slave who escaped to his freedom. A self- educated leader of the abolitionist movement in 19th century America, born in 1818.

G

Gynecologist: A medical doctor who specializes in a branch of medicine that deals with the diseases and routine physical care of the reproductive system of women.

H

Hemo-dynamics: Meaning literally "blood flow, motion and equilibrium under the action of external forces," it is the study of blood flow or the circulation. It explains the physical laws that govern the flow of blood in the blood vessels.

I

Iamsecond.com: A Christian website dedicated to the telling of how Jesus Christ has impacted the lives of people. This is a website that has an interactive portal to learn about how to accept Jesus into your heart.

Internist: A medical doctor who specializes in the diagnosis and medical treatment of adults. The specialty called Internal medicine is dedicated to adult medicine.

Intubated: Insertion of a tube into a body part, commonly used to refer to the insertion of a breathing tube into the trachea for mechanical ventilation.

Isabel Allende: Chilean journalist and Author niece of a former Chilean President. She authored a book while in exile in Venezuela called <u>The House of the Spirits</u>, born 1942.

IV pump, or infusion pump: Infuses fluids, medication or nutrients into a patient's circulatory system. It is generally used intravenously, although subcutaneous, arterial, and epidural infusions are occasionally used.

J

James Brown: American entertainer, nicknamed "the Godfather of Soul"

"Jesus, Jesus, Jesus, There's Just Something About That Name": is a Christian song copyrighted in 1970

John Milton: English poet, polemicist, man of letters, and a civil servant for the Commonwealth of England under Oliver Cromwell. He wrote at a time of religious flux and political upheaval, best known for his epic poem "Paradise Lost." Died November 8, 1674

Joseph Plumb Martin: American Soldier in the Continental Army during the American Revolution. He published a firsthand account of the life of a soldier during the American Revolution. The firsthand account is titled, Private Yankee Doodle. First published in 1830.

K

(KJV) King James Version: A version of the Holy Bible first published in 1611.

L

Lou Holtz: American Football player and coach, sports commentator, and inspirational speaker, born 1937.

Lieutenant Colonel Brian Birdwell: American Soldier, burn survivor of Pentagon attack on September 11-Texas state senator, Author of book Refined by Fire. Born 1961. Fellow burn survivor who has contributed an "I AM SECOND" video.

M

Mark Twain: American author, real name Samuel Clemens but wrote under the name Mark Twain. Literary Classics attributed to him are, _The Adventures of Tom Sawyer_ and _Huckleberry Finn_. Born in 1835.

Medal of Valor: A medal awarded for bravery, commonly called a Medal of Bravery, Bravery Medal, or Medal of Valor. A type of medal, usually associated with military forces, police forces, firemen, paramedics or other public safety entities, given to personnel who have served with gallantry, often for those who have engaged in specific acts of bravery.

Milo's Restaurant Brand: Hamburger restaurant founded in Birmingham, Alabama in 1946. Products include Hamburgers, Chicken fingers, French fries, Grilled cheese, Sweet tea, Soft drinks, and Milkshakes.

Monitor gun: A deluge gun, fire monitor, master stream, water cannon, or deck gun is a controllable high-capacity water jet used for manual firefighting or automatic fire protection systems.

N

Navy Corpsman: An enlisted medical specialist of the United States Navy who serves with the United States Navy and the United States Marine Corps.

(NLCS) National League Championship Series: in the game of baseball, the matchup that determines which team from the National League goes to the World Series.

(NIV) New International: Version of the Holy

Bible first published in 1978.

P

Pediatrician: A medical doctor who specializes in the management of the physical, behavioral, and mental health of children from birth to age 21.

Perioperative medicine: Describes the medical care of patients from the time of contemplation of surgery through the operative period to full recovery, but excludes the operation or procedure itself.

R

Remediate: A verb that means to set straight or right.

Rheumatologist: A medical doctor who specializes in the treatment of rheumatic diseases such as arthritis, lupus erythematosus, and scleroderma.

Richard Dawkins: British Evolutionary Biologist and Author. Born in Kenya 1941.

Rick Garlikov Studios: Photography studio in Birmingham Alabama. See rickgarlikov.com

Roof Truss: A structural framework designed to bridge the space above a room and to provide support for a roof.

S

Smoke inhalation: The primary cause of death for victims of indoor fires. Smoke inhalation injury refers to injury due to inhalation or exposure to hot gaseous products of combustion.

T

T4T, A Discipleship Re-Revolution: By Steve Smith and Ying Kai, a masterful guide of the simplicities of Christian Discipleship. Published in 2011. See t4tonline.org

Texas Hold'em: A form of draw poker first referenced as Hold'em in 1959, originating in the state of Texas.

The Cosby Show: An American television sitcom starring Bill Cosby, which aired for eight seasons from 1984 to 1992.

The Grove at Ole Miss: The legendary tailgating area at the center of the University of Mississippi (Ole Miss) campus. The Grove takes its name from the oak, elm, and magnolia trees surrounding the area.

Third spacing: A phenomenon that occurs when too much fluid moves from the intravascular space (blood vessels) into the interstitial or "third" space the nonfunctional area between cells. This can cause potentially serious problems such as edema, reduced cardiac output, and hypotension.

Tony Bice Memorial Golf Tournament: Proceeds from this golf tournament benefit the Children's of Alabama Burn Center which includes the UAB Hospital (University of Alabama at Birmingham) Burn Center, and the University of South Alabama Regional Burn Center

U

UAB Hospital, or University of Alabama at Birmingham Hospital: A nationally recognized leader in medical care.

UAB Spain Rehabilitation Center: One of the Southeast's foremost providers of comprehensive rehabilitation care. The center is nationally recognized.

V

Ventilator: A machine designed to mechanically move breathable air into and out of lungs to provide the mechanism of breathing for a patient who is physically unable to breathe or who is breathing insufficiently.

W

Winston Churchill: British Statesman, soldier, and prime minister of the United Kingdom during World War II. Born 1874.

WARNING

Graphic photographs of my wounds.

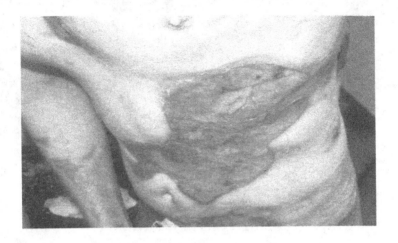

My Stomach

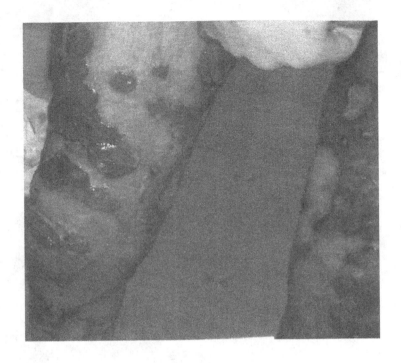

My legs

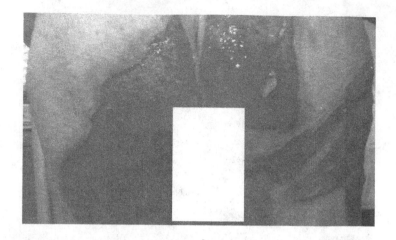

My buttocks

Bibliography

I

Milton, John. *Paradise Lost*. Oxford: Oxford University Press, 2008

II

Martin, Joseph Plumb. *Private Yankee Doodle: Being a Barative of some of the Adventures, Dangers and Sufferings of a REVOLUTIONARY SOLDIER*. Boston - Toronto: Little Brown and Company, 1962.

III

Smith, Steve. *T4T: A Discipleship Re-Revolution*. Monument, Co: WIGTake Resources, 2011.